WILL
THORNE
Constructive Militant

Will Thorne, M.P.

WILL THORNE

Constructive Militant

A Study in New Unionism
and New Politics

by

Giles and Lisanne Radice

London   George Allen & Unwin Ltd
Ruskin House   Museum Street

Printed in Great Britain
in 10/11 point Times New Roman type
by William Clowes & Sons, Limited
London, Beccles and Colchester

Dedication

To our children and all members of
the General and Municipal Workers' Union

Preface

The publication of this book is timed to coincide with the fiftieth anniversary of the 1924 amalgamation of the General Workers' Union, the National Amalgamated Union of Labour, and the Municipal Employees' Association, which created today's giant General and Municipal Workers' Union. We would like to thank David Basnett, General Secretary, and the National Executive of the GMWU for asking us to write this book and making available the Union's records.

We are also grateful to Mrs Taylor of Newham Reference library, Mrs Wagner of the Labour Party library, Miss Coates of the TUC library, the House of Commons library and the British Library of Political and Economic Science for their kindness in attending to our many requests for books, pamphlets, and unpublished documents. Lord Cooper, Sir Frederick Hayday, Lord Williamson, and George Caunt were all kind enough to discuss Will Thorne with us. We are particularly grateful to Professor Hugh Clegg with his great knowledge of the Union, and David Marquand, MP for commenting in detail on the draft of the book. We would like to thank Mrs Sheila Kapila for the trouble she took over the typing of the manuscript.

Contents

*The interests of all Workers are one, and a wrong done to
any kind of Labour is a wrong done to the whole of the
Working Class, and that victory or defeat of any portion
of the Army of Labour is a gain or a loss to the whole of
that Army, which, by its organisation and union is marching
steadily and irresistibly forward to its ultimate goal—the
Emancipation of the Working Class. That Emancipation can
only be brought about by the strenuous and united efforts
of the Working Class itself.*
    Workers Unite !

Preamble to the 1892 Rules of the National Union of
Gasworkers and General Labourers

Chapter 1

Introduction

Will Thorne's life (1857–1946) stretched from before the dawn of democratic politics to the election of the first majority Labour Government. The rise of the working-class movement that followed the widening of the franchise owed much to Thorne.

Without a doubt he was amongst the two or three leading trade unionists of his generation. He was outstanding in two ways. Though there were other trade union leaders who supported the principles of 'new unionism', Thorne was unique in his combination of aggressiveness and perseverance. Whereas Tom Mann and Ben Tillett, amongst others, shared Thorne's belief in militant trade unionism and Socialism, neither of them had quite Thorne's organisational ability or the single-minded determination necessary to sustain and develop a major union.

Thorne was also extraordinary in the sheer breadth of his achievement. Not only did he, an uneducated labourer who had been sent out to work at the age of six, create an entirely new union, the Gasworkers; but he also carried it through the difficult years until 1910, and expanded it, both through an astonishing growth in membership and by amalgamation, into the great General and Municipal Workers' Union of 1924. He was also a convinced internationalist (attending more Socialist internationals than any other trade union leader before the 1914 war), was prominent in the first Labour-controlled local authority in Britain, and, most important of all, played a vital part in the creation of the Labour Party. First elected in 1906, he combined the General Secretaryship of his union with a seat in Parliament for nearly thirty years. Stimulated by Thorne, union members and officials were exceptionally active in politics at all levels; and the Union's President, J. R. Clynes, and Chief Woman Officer, Margaret Bondfield, were ministers in both minority Labour governments of the 1920s. The following description of Thorne, though suffering

13

from hyperbole, has a ring of truth: 'He is one of the heroes of the Labour movement. When Utopia is here, some poet, making an epic of the rise of the working classes, will find his inspiration growing clearer and warmer as he approaches his canto on "Will Thorne and the Gasworkers".' [1]

By itself, Thorne's trade union work would have been enough for any one man. As a young gasworker, Thorne instinctively realised that, if the semi-skilled and unskilled labourers were to escape from their terrible working conditions, they must organise themselves into a new type of trade union. Until the 'new unionism' of 1889, sustained trade union membership was largely confined to the skilled trades and to the coal, steel, and cotton industries. Though there had been attempts to organise unskilled workers in other industries, Thorne's idea of a general union was almost entirely novel.

The Gasworkers and General Labourers' Union, created by Thorne during 1889, was distinctive in a number of ways. First it was 'new', in that it organised workers who had not previously been in trade unions. For although attempts had been made before to form a gasworkers' union, this had been mainly amongst the stokers. Thorne's union, however, included all grades. He extended his organisation to labourers in the brickworks and in a number of other industries, including local government, the woollen trades, chemicals and engineering—all of whom had had no permanent union for their type of worker before.

The variety of industries covered by his union illustrates a second characteristic—its 'general' nature. Thorne wanted the Union to be 'general', partly for the practical reason that a labourers' union with members in more than one industry would have more bargaining power and durability than one that was purely industrial, and partly because, as a Socialist, he wished to give workers, previously broken up and divided by their different industries, an opportunity to develop a new solidarity. Hence his insistence on the 'general' in the Union's full title.

Another distinguishing feature of the Gasworkers was its militancy. In order to unite the workers and to force the employers to recognise his union, Thorne, in the early years, used the strike weapon on many occasions. His insistence that the Gasworkers should be 'a fighting union' meant, at least in the beginning, a refusal to introduce—with the exception of strike pay—the many benefits which were so much a feature of craft unionism. Though, in periods of high unemployment, Thorne adopted a more

14

pragmatic attitude to strikes, he was never frightened to use trade union power in a just cause—provided it was not to the detriment of his members.

Finally, from the beginning, the Gasworkers' Union had definite political and social aims. Thorne's membership of the Social Democratic Federation, the first British Socialist group, was an important influence on the character of the new union. The previous generation of trade union leaders had been Lib-Labers, content to work through the existing political system, and their objectives had, therefore, been limited. As a result of his political commitment, Thorne always saw industrial problems in a wider context. He was convinced that it was impossible to make radical improvements in the living standards of his members without changing the political and social system. It was Thorne whom Engels had in mind when, surveying the British trade union scene, he wrote to Laura Lafargue, daughter of Karl Marx: 'These new trade unions of unskilled men are totally different from the old organisations of the working-class aristocracy and cannot fall into the same conservative ways . . . they are organised under quite different circumstances. . . . In them I see the *real* beginning of the movement here.' [2]

In one sense, Engels was right. For the logical consequence of Thorne's Socialism was trade union participation in politics—an involvement, which, by the end of the 1890s, because of the employers' counterattack against the unions, both directly and through the courts, had become even more necessary. Thorne realised, from the start, that the only hope of change was for the workers to set up their own independent party—preferably one committed to a Socialist programme. In the years after 1894, part of his energy was, therefore, concentrated on the creation of a new political force.

The Gasworkers' contribution under Will Thorne to the Labour Party, both locally and nationally, cannot be overestimated. Thorne, himself, was an innovator in local government. Nationally, the role of Thorne as the vital linkman between the trade unions and the Socialist groups in the negotiations leading up to the formation of the Labour Representation Committee in 1900 has not been sufficiently emphasised by historians. In the years before the 1914–18 war, Thorne and other Gasworker officials, including J. R. Clynes and Pete Curran, played an important part in the development of the Labour Party, both in Parliament and outside.

At a superficial level, it is possible to argue that the 1914–18 war blunted the sharpness of Thorne's radicalism. Thorne, like the majority of the British Labour Movement, supported the war effort. The former internationalist spoke on recruitment platforms up and down the country, and became more of an Establishment figure.

Yet the record of the Gasworkers, under Thorne and Clynes, the Union's president, both during the war and in the years immediately after it was impressive enough. During the war, the Gasworkers' Union dramatically extended its membership amongst the semi-skilled and unskilled in many industries but particularly in the munitions factories—so much so that, in 1916, the Union's name was changed to the General Workers' Union. The Union became one of the champions of women workers, helping to win equal pay for women employed on men's jobs in munitions factories. It also put its full weight behind the cause of the low paid, even threatening a national strike if they were not given an equivalent increase to the one awarded to the skilled workers. With the other general unions, the General Workers' Union exploited its new bargaining power to set up a system of national negotiations in a number of important industries. By 1920, the general unions, with Thorne's union at their head, were a real force for the first time—and added very considerably to the strength of the trade union movement.

After the war, Thorne and Clynes stood out against the use of the strike as a political weapon except over British intervention in the Russo-Polish war, because of their faith in parliamentary democracy. Clynes, himself, had been a successful Food Controller in the Lloyd George wartime coalition, helping to control food prices and stop speculation—a great benefit to his own members. After 1918, both Thorne and Clynes believed that a Labour government was a strong possibility in the near future and that such shortcuts as direct action would, in nearly all cases, only help the forces of reaction. Though the two minority Labour governments, of which Clynes was a prominent member, were disappointments (particularly that of 1929–31), Thorne remained, as he had always been, a convinced believer in Democratic Socialism. It is entirely appropriate that he should have lived to see the formation of the first majority Labour government which carried through many of the measures for which he had fought.

Thorne's last great service to his union was the amalgamation of 1924, which created today's General and Municipal Workers'

Union. Amalgamation of unions had been one of his earliest objectives. He always believed it wrong that workers should be divided from each other by the particular interests of their different organisations. However, it was only under the pressure of mass unemployment and falling trade union membership that he was able to bring off the amalgamation of major labourers' unions, for which he had worked so long. He failed to bring in the Workers' Union; but against this must be set his achievement of persuading first, the National Federation of Woman Workers and the Birmingham Gasworkers at the end of 1920 and, then, in 1924, the much larger National Amalgamated Union of Labour and the potentially important Municipal Employees' Association to submerge their separate identities in a larger grouping.

It would have been better if Thorne had retired in 1924. Instead, his union allowed him to continue too long as General Secretary—until 1933 when he was seventy-six years old. But his later years cannot detract from his greatness as a trade union leader.

Chapter 2

Early Life

Will Thorne was born in Birmingham in 1857, six years after the Great Exhibition, at a time when Britain's predominance over the world seemed unchallenged and her social stability assured. The Crimean War had been won, and Lord Palmerston, the living symbol of British superiority, had triumphed in the general election of that year; small wonder that the middle and upper classes felt that 'a sense of satisfaction permeates the country, because most of the country feels it has got the precise thing which suits it'.[1] Looking to the future, there was no reason for these classes to doubt that Britain would course through the last half of the nineteenth century even more successfully than in the past. Secure in her industrial might and in her constitution, mercifully untouched by revolution, the years ahead could only bring to the nation further prosperity. Even the working class uplifted, it was hoped, by the improving philosophy of Samuel Smiles, would, in its turn, attain its own modicum of affluence.

However, the comfortable assumptions of the upper and middle classes about Britain's and their own future were over optimistic. British superiority was challenged by the growth of new industrial powers, economic progress became more uncertain, and the aspirations of the working class began to grow. If the life of Robert Applegarth, President of the Amalgamated Society of Carpenters and Joiners, exemplified the attitude of the trade unions up to the middle years of the nineteenth century,[2] that of Will Thorne could well serve as a symbol of their different mood at the end of Victoria's reign. Applegarth, respected artisan, conciliatory negotiator, and political moderate and Thorne, unskilled labourer, militant striker, and convinced Socialist, were prototypes of their respective ages. The former hoped that his members would 'become respectful and respected'; the latter, speaking the language of class war, determined to lift himself and

18

his fellow workmen 'out of the slime of poverty into the fresh air of freedom'.[3] The shift in trade union objectives which Thorne both symbolised and helped to create was to change the face of British industrial and political life.

Will Thorne's introduction to industrial action came at an early age. Sent out to full-time work at the age of six, his first job was turning a wheel for a rope and twine spinner. He earned 2s 6d a week for a 12-hour day, with $1\frac{1}{2}$ hours allowed for his breakfast and dinner. It was in this, his earliest employment, that, as he puts it, 'I experienced my first strike. It was a brief one, over 6d a week, and occurred when the spinner I worked for at the Rope Walk wanted to reduce my wages from 2s 6d per week to 2s per week. I refused to accept this reduction and went on strike. But that strike was never settled and I never returned.'[4] He may not have won, but he had shown, when only a small child, that he was prepared to fight for his rights.

His father died (as a result of a drunken brawl) when he was seven, leaving him and his mother to provide for the three younger children. There was never any question of his having time to go to school. The Thorne family was so destitute that it even had to apply for Poor Relief which Will collected once a week, walking the extra four miles each Wednesday on top of his usual day's work. He was by then employed in a brick and tile works, 'leaving home at 4.30 walking four miles to work, and then, after a long twelve-hour day, walking back again, a fifteen-hour day by the time I got home, dead tired, barely able to eat my scanty tea and crawl into bed.'[5]

From making bricks, Will Thorne went to a Birmingham ammunitions factory. It was during the Franco-Prussian War and the munition works were in full production, with urgent orders from both the French and the Germans to fulfil. And it was here that he learnt one of his 'earliest lessons in the law of supply and demand'.[6] The strip and metal rollers employed in the factory struck for an advance; and so great was the pressure for orders that the firm gave way and granted higher wages. However, this job ended, as had his first, with the sack. Once more his employers decided on a cut in his wages, and once more he went on strike. It is a tribute to Thorne's self-confidence that he had come out on strike a total of five times before he had turned eighteen.

As he grew older, Will Thorne's employment assumed a more

regular pattern. He remained a general labourer, but worked in the gasworks in the winter and, when the labourers were laid off, with the brick- and tile-making companies in the summer. He, therefore, experienced directly the considerable difficulties of seasonal employment.

Thorne's first success as an organiser came when he worked as a stoker at the Saltley gasworks in Birmingham. He put in a daily twelve-hour shift, drawing and charging the retorts in conditions of such unbearable heat, that it was almost impossible for the men to stand in front of the furnace for long before getting their boots burnt off. Thorne objected to the twenty-four hour shift which the stokers had to work on Sundays to complete the changeover to a new shift the following Monday morning. What he wanted was the abolition of Sunday work to lessen the inhuman working conditions, and, with this in mind, he set out to persuade his fellow stokers to send a deputation to the works management. It was a task he found surprisingly difficult; the men were apathetic and 'put up all sorts of arguments against my proposals, but I stuck to them. "It seems," I said, "that you think more about the lives of the retorts than you do about your own lives." This remark had the right effect.'[7] The men 'plucked up courage' and agreed to send a deputation, if Thorne would do all the arguing for them. The result, after a certain amount of abuse from the management, and a special visit from Joseph Chamberlain (the then Mayor of Birmingham Corporation) to check for himself as to the conditions, was a settlement in favour of the stokers.

Although he had found it difficult to persuade the men to speak up even for their own cause, he was determined that, having won the day, the victory should be followed up by the formation of a union which would demand 'a reduction in the working hours, for I knew that, with such a reduction more men would be employed, our labour would become more valuable and our economic and industrial strength greater'.[8] Though nothing came of his agitation because of the men's fear of dismissal and their general apathy, Thorne had hit on a platform which, because it was simple and answered a real need, was to be a vital ingredient in the formation of the Gasworkers' Union.

He did not, however, remain long in the Saltley gasworks. The Birmingham Corporation, anxious to reduce expenditure, introduced a new machine for drawing and charging the retorts at the works. Known as the 'iron man', it was worked by compressed air and replaced the old rakes and shovels which had been previously used to charge the retorts with coal and to draw off the coke. Unfortunately for the employees, it had three disadvantages. It increased the speed with which the stokers had to work, so that often they had no time even to eat their food between charges; it frequently broke down, with no extra time given for repairs; and it could be worked by two men instead of four. It was this final saving by the Corporation which stimulated Will Thorne's second protest at the gasworks. Once more a meeting was held, and this time it was agreed that the men should come out on strike. The results were double edged; working conditions were improved; however, the strikers, including Thorne, were dismissed. More than his sacking, the men's apparent reluctance to better their own conditions affected him deeply. Discussing it later, he wrote bitterly of that strike. 'there are lots of workers too cowardly to stand by their comrades in fighting for their rights, but who are always prepared to accept any advantage won by them'.[9]

His dismissal from the Saltley gasworks in 1881 was to change his life. Thorne decided that, although it would mean leaving behind a pregnant wife and young baby, he would walk to London to look for work there. Will Thorne was twenty-four when he decided to go south. What, up to this time, had been the main influences in his life? Sacked at six for refusing a reduction in his wages, dismissed at nine for sleeping on his job at 4 a.m. (having that week worked two days and nights without a break), humpbacked from heaving bricks into kilns, he had had an early introduction to the horrors of industrial life that he never forgot. His future philosophy was to be based on those early experiences of long hours, no childhood, and work in surroundings where 'the roar and rattle, the steam and the heat of that inferno remained vivid in my memory, and many times I have dreamt of the place, waking up in a cold sweat of fear'.[10] Brutalising work in the factory, sweated labour and Poor Relief at home for his widowed mother, these remained indelibly marked on his character. For Will Thorne, born before the Education Acts of the 1870s, there was never to be any question of schooling; indeed, so neglected had his education been, that when he married in 1879, he could only make his 'mark' on the marriage certificate. Unlike Clynes, the other great figure in the Gasworkers' Union, Will Thorne never had the time, nor indeed, the inclination, for study. Writing many years later about the influences in his life which had helped him form his own personal philosophy, he put personal contact far ahead of any theoretical works he was later to study. Even in his understanding of ideological questions more important to him than their books 'was the personal contact I had with great thinkers, and working class leaders like Karl Liebknecht, Herr Bebel and Singer, Dr Adler and Frederick Engels of Germany; Paul Lafargue and the wonderful Jean Jaurès, of France'.[11]

The most notable feature of Thorne's early life was the remarkable confidence he displayed in himself and in the working classes. Much of this must have come from within himself. However, Thorne believed that one of the most formative experiences was working with the 'navvies' on the construction of the Burton and Derby railway line. 'I am sure,' he wrote, 'that the days I spent in the open air, working as a navvy, living with these big-hearted carefree men, and absorbing their conversation, had much to do with my future. They were an independent type, with the spark of rebellion glowing bright within them.'[12] What struck him forcibly was that these men, as opposed to the labourers with whom he had worked in factories and gasworks, were neither afraid of their masters, nor apathetic about their rights. It was just this kind of attitude that Thorne longed to see emerge among the unskilled workers who seemed afraid to strike even when their pay was reduced and their hours increased. Such a way of thinking, he believed, could best be achieved if the men were organised in their own, powerful trade unions.

Will Thorne arrived in London in November 1881, and sought a job in the gasworks—a good time to find employment, as it was the beginning of the winter and the demand for labourers at its height. It is also worth noting that Thorne, though an unskilled labourer, chose to find work at the Old Kent Road Gasworks, not only because he knew a workman there but also because he must have thought of himself as something of a 'specialist' in the gas industry—a 'skilled' gasworker (even though he worked as a brick labourer during the summer). Historians of the 'new unionism'[13] have claimed that the early leaders of the general unions were less unskilled than had been previously thought, and, to this extent, Thorne's specialisation in an unskilled job, that of stoking, bears them out. His first job in the London gasworks was not, however, that of a stoker; it was pulling coke barrows from the stokers, taking the red hot coke into an open yard, throwing water on it, and then stacking it into a heap. He might originally have been employed because of his past experiences as a stoker, but the job he was given could have been done by any unskilled labourer.

Thorne's first job in London lasted a short time. He was dismissed when certain retorts were closed down at the beginning of summer; as he had been one of the last to be employed, he was one of the first to be dismissed. It was a bitter blow to him, for, by then, he had brought his wife and baby down from Birmingham and his wife had had another daughter. There was nothing he could do but return to the Midlands, so that at least his wife and children could live with her parents. Once more he found employment in the Saltley gasworks. But, as on the previous occasion, not for long. The same crisis situation arose as had before; the men were told to increase their productivity for the same wages, and, once more, Will Thorne agitated for, and was successful in calling a strike. But, again, the 'dumb dogs' as he angrily called his fellow workmen, refused to give him wholehearted support. For the second time, and this time for good, Thorne found himself making the long journey back to London by foot.

He found another job at the Beckton gasworks in West Ham, one, which because of the awkward construction of the retort house, was harder and hotter than any in which he had previously been employed. He sent for his wife once more, and moved into lodgings in Canning Town, hoping that this would be his last move. His wages at this time were 5s 4d a day, which was too meagre a sum, he felt, to allow him any extras. So, on 8 September 1885, Will Thorne signed a

TEMPERANCE PLEDGE
I promise by Divine Assistance to abstain
from all intoxicating Liquors and Beverages.
Signed William Thorne
Thomas Tugg (Visitor)[14]

Samuel Smiles would have been proud of him!

Besides becoming a teetotaller, Thorne had already taken another step. In the year of the Third Reform Act, he joined the local branch of the Social Democratic Federation. The SDF had been founded in 1881 by H. M. Hyndman, a leading British Marxist, and was the first organised Socialist society. Its initial platform was for a 'social and political programme which shall unite the great body of the people, quite irrespective of party'.[15]

Unhappily it suffered from much internal strife, tended to be dogmatic and sectarian in character, and failed to attract, unlike its later rival, the Independent Labour Party, any significant part of the working class, so that Thorne as an unskilled labourer, was something of an anomaly in the movement. Its revolutionary programme included nationalisation of all 'means of production, distribution and exchange', the eight-hour working day, free elementary education, payment of Members of Parliament, and the abolition of a standing army and the establishment in its place of a National Citizen Force. It also recommended the use of the referendum for major legislative measures. Thorne's membership of the SDF affected his whole way of thinking, and, thus, influenced considerably the development of the trades union movement. The leading trade unionists of the eighties were men who were, on the whole, satisfied with the existing political system, and perfectly content with the trade union movement to be allied with the Liberal Party in Parliament. Thorne, as a member of the SDF, provided a new kind of leadership, Socialist and militant; and this different approach was an important factor in both the emergence of the new unions and of the Labour Party.

It is clear that Thorne owed a great deal to his membership of the SDF. His participation in the local Canning Town branch gave him a confidence, based on firmly held political beliefs, that was to sustain him when he particularly needed it—at the time of the formation of his union. The Socialist idea of working-class unity in the face of capitalist oppression not only strengthened him personally but also gave him an additional, and, in some ways, a more powerful argument when it came to trade union organisation.

He gained other advantages from his SDF membership. Although Thorne had obviously from early on been involved in workplace meetings, it is clear from his autobiography that it was not until he joined the SDF that he became expert in debate and crowd oratory—an invaluable tool for a trade union leader. From the moment that he became a member, he participated in constant public meetings, distributing Socialist literature and persuading his often reluctant fellow operatives to throw off their lassitude and work for the cause of Socialism. For a short time, he became the Secretary of the Canning Town Branch, in which capacity he met Tom Mann, who impressed him enormously, and George Bernard Shaw, whom he found difficult to understand. He was also introduced to Edward Aveling, Harry Quelch, John Ward, and John Burns, thinkers and propagandists who strengthened him in his Socialism. Perhaps most important of all, he got to know Karl Marx's daughter, Eleanor Marx Aveling, who was to help him found his union, to become a member of his Executive Committee, and to teach him to write correctly. He learnt quickly, and his organisational and political abilities were soon noticed. W. S. Sanders, one time Secretary of the Fabian Society, reminiscing many years later, described the effect Thorne had on him when he first met him during this period at a political meeting. The latter had come straight out onto the platform 'from the retort house with the murk of the fiery place burnt into his features. Round his eyes were dark rings of coal-grime, and his hands were, and are still, gnarled and knotted by the handling of the charging tools. His voice, as I remember it, was not strong, and his words were not eloquent, but his obvious sincerity was more convincing than fine phrases. . . . To the persistence and the loyalty to their class on the part of Will Thorne and his union colleagues, who have combined Socialist fervour with common-sense and patience, are largely due the improvement that has taken place in the status and outlook of the masses who are outside the ranks of the mechanic and craftsman.' [16]

Thorne's association with the SDF was not only useful in practical terms. His belief in Socialism was to influence his whole way of thinking. While it is clear that he founded his union on the basis of his own experiences in the gas- and brick-making industries, his decision to make it general in character was also a reflection of his Socialist philosophy. A union that would cater for all would increase the strength of working-class solidarity and bring nearer that time when a new industrial and political struggle could be waged against the power of the employers. The unions would provide the necessary base from which a new political party could be launched which would be both fully representative of the working classes and committed to Socialist aims. He did not, however, believe in a violent revolution on the Marxist model, having come to the conclusion, after reading J. Sketchley's book on *A Review of European Society, and an Exposition and Vindication of the Principles of Social Democracy*, that it was through Parliament that the dreadful conditions of the working classes would be changed. 'I was convinced,' he wrote, 'that radical changes would have to be made, and the franchise for men and women broadened, and to these ends I devoted some of my propaganda efforts.' [17]

The late eighties were years of political agitation and mass

25

meetings. The SDF ran Sunday rallies which the police tried to stop; meetings were broken up and speakers arrested. The police, however, soon realised that the arrests merely advertised the presence of the Socialists and began to leave them alone. To celebrate their victory, the SDF organised a mass demonstration, one of the largest ever held, at the West India Dock Gates on the Sunday of 27 September 1885. Over 50,000 people came to hear the speakers. It was an impressive occasion, followed up by further similar meetings held in different parts of London, as far apart as Chelsea and Enfield. It was an excellent initiation period for Will Thorne; he learnt the practicalities and difficulties of speaking to a mass audience and to define and express clearly his objectives.

Unemployment grew, and so did the agitation; meetings were held up and down the country to demand government help for the unemployed. And it was at one of these mass rallies that Thorne had his first experience of crowd hysteria. The meeting, held on 8 February 1886, and later known as 'Black Monday', took place in a packed Trafalgar Square with orators speaking from different platforms. The SDF passed a resolution that the unemployment problem should be tackled by a programme of public works, especially housing, and by the shortening of the working hours of the transport workers. The crowd around its platform, excited by the oratory of the SDF leaders, marched down Pall Mall, John Burns in the lead waving a red flag. The sight of the Reform Club, filled with members who seemed to be jeering at the crowds, was too much for the workers; they broke ranks and, in retaliation, began smashing the club windows and breaking into the shops along the street. The result was the inevitable arrests of Burns, Champion, Hyndman, and Jack Williams, all of whom had spoken at the meeting, on charges of sedition. Their trial, which was used as a public platform by the defendants, ended in acquittal.

The prosecution failed to deter Will Thorne, who continued to be involved in political agitation. A year later, he was once more caught in yet another great mass demonstration, this time called to protest against the coercion powers of the government. As marchers began to converge from all parts of London to the central rallying point of Trafalgar Square, it became clear that the police had every intention of breaking the meeting up. Thorne's branch of the SDF had hired a two-horse brake to drive the members to the meeting, but so great were the crowds that, long before they reached Trafalgar Square, they had to disembark and go on foot.

It was a frightening experience for, when 'we arrived at Wellington Street, Strand, policemen were streched four deep across the road. We were within a few yards of the cordon when the policemen, at a command, drew their truncheons and made a charge at us. It was a ferocious onslaught.' [18] Thorne got off lightly, receiving a nasty tap on the head, but others were more seriously injured, with one member of the Socialist League later dying of his wounds. Burns and Cunningham-Graham, the Radical MP for North-West Lanark who had recently become a Socialist, were arrested and sent to prison.

The unrest continued, as the employment situation worsened. Apart from political agitation, Will Thorne helped more directly. The unemployment crisis had especially affected his own neighbourhood of West Ham, with the areas round the docks in Canning Town, Tidal Basin and Custom House being particularly hard hit by the continued recession. With their men often out of work for months at a time, many women and children were starving. In an attempt to alleviate the suffering, Thorne, with the support of a few comrades, set up soup kitchens in a temperance bar at 144 Barking Road. He did not exaggerate their effectiveness, but the sight of the starving children who anxiously queued up for their food impressed him so deeply that he vowed that a system 'that permitted the poor to starve in the East End while in the West End others satisfied their appetites with luxurious meals amidst the greatest comfort,' [19] would have to be destroyed.

By the end of 1887, therefore, Will Thorne had been involved in agitation on both political and industrial fronts. Initially interested in improving conditions of work, he had begun, through his active membership of the SDF, to evolve his own political philosophy and to see industrial problems in the wider context of political and social change. Both, he believed, hinged on each other. And as he became accustomed to mass meetings, so he grew increasingly skilful in public argument and debate, his confidence grew and his ideas clarified. This new-found stature was to stand him in good stead when he began the difficult task of forming his own union.

Chapter 3

The 'New Union'

Thorne's was not the first attempt to start a union in the gas industry in London. A gas stokers' union had been founded as early as 1872, but the leaders had been convicted as a result of a strike and the union had faded. Some twelve years later, a further attempt was made by a London gasworker, Jack Monk, but the strength of the employers was so great that the members, afraid of victimisation, met only in the greatest secrecy and the union came to nothing. A third bid came in the next year, led by a friend of Will Thorne's, George Angle, with the union headquarters in Canning Town, but once more fear of the employers led to its demise after a few months.

Despite the latest set back, Thorne continued to agitate, as he had in Birmingham, for the formation of a union. He felt that the times were more favourable, as the recession of the middle 1880s had changed into a period of expansion. His belief in Socialism and his innate conviction in the need for trade unions pushed Thorne into determined and sustained agitation both inside and outside the factory gates. 'I had a goal, an aim, a message.' [1] He even attempted, unsuccessfully, to convert the resident engineer of the gasworks to his Socialist creed, subjecting him to a dramatic harangue. 'I stood with my foot on a pile of coal, with the flashing lights of the retorts athwart the paper, and above the noise of the works I declaimed John Burns' words.' [2] Management may have held aloof, but Thorne soon found that he had a small following amongst the workers.

These early months of agitation and discussion in the Beckton gasworks were vital, for they set the pattern for Thorne's future activities. He decided to concentrate on trade union organisation. Political changes were necessary, but, he felt, that the 'need for these changes and reforms was, however, not as pressing as those demanding attention in the workshop, for here the employers

28

were rapidly creating the conditions that were giving the workers only the alternative of servile submission to tyranny of the worst kind and abject wage slavery, or of uniting in some form of combination.' [3] And, having made his decision, Thorne, although never giving up his political work, relegated it to second place, even when he became a Member of Parliament and a West Ham Councillor.

His hopes of forming a union suddenly turned into reality. The Beckton Gas Company decided to introduce the 'iron man' into their works. It was natural that Will Thorne, who had been sacked because of this very innovation in Birmingham, should protest against it once more. Immediately the 'iron man' was installed, Thorne was told, probably because it was known that he had previous experience, that he would have to work on it. He resented the new machinery because it made for a reduction in the number of men employed, and because he felt, as he had in Birmingham, that the work demanded of the men was too much. He explained the likely difficulties to his fellow workers and was appointed to make representations to the foreman; the latter, however, refused to listen to the workers' complaints. Thorne told the workers that they would have to accept management's terms but cleverly made it clear that the only reason for their failure was that 'they had no union behind them'. [4]

As at Saltley, so at Beckton; the machines began to break down, the men were forced to put in extra time in which to mend them, and the work became harder than it had been when they had had to stoke by hand. However, at Beckton, further innovations were introduced. Each meter house was checked hourly for the cubic capacity of gas it produced; and any which made less than the others had to speed up its gas production. Another method of increasing gas output was also brought into practice. The retorts were usually charged ten times during the day and ten times through the night. The system employed was for five charges to be made, to be followed by a long rest, and then the further five would be completed. The gas company now instructed the foremen to speed up the five early charges so that time would be made for one more charge to be worked before the long rest.

Even though the working conditions deteriorated rapidly, Will Thorne was almost alone in his agitation to have them changed. It was only when yet another innovation was introduced that he managed to persuade the men to 'down tools'. A new practice was instituted whereby some men on the Sunday shift were asked to stay on to make three extra charges on top of their previous work. Not only did they have to work an eighteen-hour shift instead of twelve, but, because the workers concerned never knew when they would have to stay on, they brought no extra food. As a result, most workers had to walk the four miles back to their homes hungry and exhausted. 'They were almost prepared to go on strike, even though they had no union behind them. I saw the time was ripe; the day that I had waited for so long had at last dawned. This was the psychological moment for forming the Union.' [5]

To challenge the new eighteen-hour shift, Will Thorne chose Sunday 31 March 1889 to hold a meeting in Canning Town of his fellow workmen. His purpose was to launch a gasworkers' union and to demand an eight-hour day. Thorne organised the meeting brilliantly; he not only had his own contingent of men preceded by a noisy band, but he also had invited on the platform with him such crowd drawers as Ben Tillett, Harry Hobart, and other members of the SDF. He appealed to the men, not only to form a union, but to make it general in character, begging them, meanwhile, to stand firm against the employers. 'Stand together this time; forget the past efforts we have made to form you into a union. . . . Some of you were afraid of your own shadows, but this morning I want you to swear and declare that you mean business and that nothing will deter you from your aim.' [6]

There was no hesitation that morning. A committee was formed and eight hundred new members tossed their entrance fee of one shilling into hastily borrowed buckets. Payments continued to flow in, so that by the end of two weeks the union had over 3,000 members. The new union's programme—to work for the establishment of an eight-hour day—had gained substantial support. A provisional committee was set up to organise meetings all over London, to draw up a set of rules, and to decide on the amount of contributions to be paid. From the start, Thorne made it clear that what he wanted was a different kind of organisation to that of the craft unions; hence his insistence on very low union contributions. The new union was named the National Union of Gasworkers and General Labourers, the contribution was the nominal sum of twopence, and the motto was 'One Man, one Ticket, and every Man with a Ticket'.

The Union quickly began to acquire a more permanent character. Within a few weeks, rules were submitted to a delegate meeting; it was decided to appoint a General Secretary with a weekly salary of 45s; and, instead of asking for an increase of a shilling a day which some of the members had wanted as the Union's main claim, the meeting agreed to Thorne's demand for an eight-hour day. By the end of June, the Gasworkers had successfully negotiated the introduction of an eight-hour shift in the London gasworks. The employers had been defeated by unpreparedness and by their inability to find men to replace those who might come out on strike at short notice; equally important, the solidarity of the workers had proved crucial. By 1 June 1889, Thorne, against whom Ben Tillett had stood, 'not because of any ill-feeling against me but because of his knowledge of clerical and bookkeeping work',[7] was overwhelmingly voted in as the Union's first General Secretary.

Although the gas company did not increase the number of its stokers by a third (as might have been expected under the new three-shift system), the success of the Gasworkers' Union 'put heart into thousands of unskilled, badly paid and unorganised workers'.[8] The appreciation of the members of Will Thorne's efforts was immediately expressed. On 17 July 1889, a concert was organised by the men working on the newly established No. 3 shift at the Beckton gasworks; and the Union's first General Secretary was presented with a silver watch and chain and an address thanking him for the tireless energy with which he had pursued his objectives. It was, he said 'particularly pleasing that the happy little function was promoted by the No. 3 shift, because under the twelve-hour day there had only been two shifts'.[9] For Thorne the formation of the Union 'was the definite establishment, and the beginning of ... 'New Unionism'. It was the culmination of long years of Socialist propaganda amongst the underpaid and oppressed workers. Politics had been preached to them as vague and indefinite appeals to revolution, but we offered them something tangible, a definite, clearly lighted road out of their misery, a trade union that would improve their wages and conditions; that would protect them from the petty tyranny of employers.'[10]

Why were the gasworkers successfully organised in 1889? According to Thorne, the reasons why the gasworkers, after months of hesitation, agreed to form a union, were the accumulated dislike of management decisions, the introduction of the 'iron man', the resulting increase in the tempo at which the shifts worked, and the sudden and apparently arbitrary demands of the employers that some of the men should work an eighteen-hour shift on Sundays. This was a combination of factors that had never previously coincided. As historians have rightly argued, the actual introduction of mechanisation was not the major cause of the dispute.[11] However, allied to other grievances, it became one of the key factors in the crucial Beckton strike. Equally important, this was an era of full employment and expansion in the gas industry (the number of gasworkers increased from 14,000 in 1861 to 45,000 in 1891),[12] so that any organised strike action had the maximum impact, especially as the gas companies, because of their commitment to the public, could not afford too long or costly a fight. There was another contributory cause to the success of the gasworkers. Once conditions were right, the gas industry was easier to organise than had previously been realised. Although the gasworkers were employed on a seasonal basis, in practice the same men (as in the case of Thorne) were reemployed season after season. This meant that the labourers knew each other and a hard core (though small in number) of union-orientated men, on whom also the steady output of gas depended, were taken on every year in the London gasworks.

Thorne's character and personality, and the quality of leadership he provided, were also of the greatest importance in the successful development of the Union. He was not only a gasworker of long standing, and, therefore, knowledgeable about the industry, but, by 1889, he had been involved with the Socialist movement for five years and had become an experienced speaker and organiser. These early London years, as has been mentioned, proved crucial to his development. The fact that he had Socialist backing, with the Avelings, in particular, to guide him, added to the unformed aspirations of his Birmingham days a new sharpness and dimension. His Socialism strengthened his belief in the need for industrial action and his friendship with such diverse figures as Shaw, Tillett, Hyndman, and Engels stimulated him in his desire to found a trade union. No doubt too, Eleanor Marx, as she taught him to write correctly and to keep his union books, also encouraged him in his difficult task.

But, apart from his organisational abilities, Thorne had another strength. He was a man much admired and looked up to by his fellow workers and union members—a natural leader. Lansbury, who met him for the first time when the Gasworkers' Union was in the process of being formed, was immediately so attracted to

32

him that he joined his own local branch of the Union,[13] while
G. D. H. Cole, who also knew him well, was later to write of him
that he 'owed his influence to his entire single-minded honesty
and devotion and to his immence capacity for hard work'.[14] His
own men expressed themselves more fervently. He was, they said,
a 'Champion of the Rights of Labour, from his boyhood, his
Untiring Energy, his Manly Courage, his earnest Advocacy, and
his Honesty of Purpose in the Cause of Trade Unionism, has
gained for him Admiration and Respect of all ranks in the Army
of Labour'.[15]

What was it about the Gasworkers that differentiated them
from the existing craft unions? Three distinguishing characteris-
tics have been generally attributed to the new unions of the 1890s:
'newness, general organisation and militancy.'[16] How far were
these applicable to Thorne's Union?

Certainly, the Gasworkers' Union had the characteristic of
newness, for, although some attempts had previously been made
to organise gasworkers, Thorne's bid in the March of 1889 was
the first successful one. Thorne, himself, although a member of
Tillett's Tea Operatives and General Labourers' Association, felt
that a new union would best serve the interests of the labourers in
the gasworks. The Union was also new in the type of labourer
whom it hoped to attract, for, although the stokers, the original
hard core of the membership, might be regarded by their employers as having a semi-skilled capacity, Thorne himself thought
otherwise. He believed that the management would not find it
difficult to find replacements in time of strikes, and was therefore
anxious to include every worker, from yard labourer to stoker,
within the Union. With Tillett and Mann, he believed that the
'organisation of those who are classed as unskilled is of the most
vital importance, and must receive adequate attention; no longer
can the skilled assume with a sort of superior air that they are the
salt of the earth'.[17]

The characteristic of newness was closely related to the kind of
organisation that Thorne believed he was setting up. It is true that
the Union was not as general as he had hoped, and that membership was, on the whole, confined to industries, such as gas and
other municipal services, which provided stable employment; but
the fact remains that Thorne considered that he was attracting the
general labourer, hence his determination on the low contribution
of 2d a week. What he wished to achieve was a union which,
though it might initially be based on men in regular employment

in the gas industry, would eventually take in any unskilled labourer. It was with this in mind that, from the first, he insisted on the title of The Gasworkers and General Labourers' Union.

If there is some controversy over the 'general' character of the new unions, there can be less over the distinctive aims of their organisation. The old craft unions had offered their members attractive benefits, but Thorne, like other leaders of the new unions, utterly rejected the idea that the distribution of benefits should be the main objective of a union. He spoke out against them from the beginning, and, when criticised for his attitude, he replied firmly. 'I do not,' he wrote, 'believe in having sick pay, out of work pay, and a number of other pays, we desire to prevent so much sickness and men being out of work. The way to accomplish this, is firstly to organise, then reduce your hours of labour or work, that will prevent illness and members being out of employment.' [18] To him, the only benefit that mattered was that of strike pay and, although the single benefit system did not last long, as various districts (which were more or less autonomous) demanded and were granted the right to have sickness and burial benefits, Thorne's acceptance of these was more a modification than a fundamental change in attitude.

The militancy which marked the new unions was much commented on by later historians, and it was certainly a feature of the Gasworkers' Union from the start. Thorne realised that, because unskilled labourers lacked the scarcity value of the craftsmen, the only way they could bring pressure to bear on the employers was to withdraw their labour. In the first years of the Union's existence, Thorne used the strike weapon on many occasions, both to give force to his members' demands and to attract new members. However, for a strike to be successful, it was essential that the men should be united and that all the workers should come out on strike. Thorne was, therefore, insistent on trying to create 'closed shops' so that a strike could not be undermined by blacklegs—a strategy that was often interpreted by the union's enemies as intimidation and likely to lead to violence.

Thorne's use of the strike—and the threat of a strike—as a weapon in negotiation was due not only to his desire to strengthen his members' bargaining power but was also bound up with his Socialist philosophy. The greetings sent on behalf of the Executive of the Gasworkers to the International Miners' Congress held in 1891 goes far in explaining his attitude. It was a straightforward appeal to 'our Brothers, the miners of all nations, to our fellow workers who whilst speaking in tongues different from ours, are one with us in belonging to the oppressed and exploited class; are one with us in the great class struggle of Labour against capitalists; and one with us in the determination that the struggle shall have but one end—the emancipation of the working class—to you, our Brothers, "Courage, Unity, Hope!".' [19]

It should not be forgotten that Thorne's Gasworkers believed strongly that trade unionism had to be seen in a wider social and political context. They demanded a fairer distribution of wealth and a more just society. In particular, Thorne urged his members to put pressure on the government for an enlightened state educational policy. In his first report, he pointed out to his members that because shorter working hours had been achieved they now had a better opportunity to obtain some further education 'which is one of the greatest blessings a man can possess' for when 'men are better educated they become sensible of the manner in which they have been deprived of the results of their labours'.[20] Thorne also believed that, without an independent political party representative of the working class, there could be no progress. Thus the Gasworkers' concern with political and social objectives and their demand for a genuine independent workers' party also distinguished them from the old unions.

Within six months of that first March meeting, Thorne's Union had 20,000 members, by July 1889 sixty branches had been established (forty-four in London); and, during that same year, the General Secretary, with his growing reputation, helped to direct the successful London dock strike. Thorne never let up in those months, travelling round his new districts, helping set up different branches, explaining the rules and policies of the Union, and never forgetting, so he tells us, to preach good Socialist propaganda.[21]

It was the success of the Gasworkers' Union that inspired the dockers to form a union of their own. The dockers, themselves, approached Thorne asking to join his union, but, instead, he sent them to his friend Ben Tillett whose Tea Operatives and Dock Workers' Union had been in existence for some time; it was a gesture of friendship towards, and a solidarity with, a man who had helped him to found his own union. However, on 10 August 1889, Thorne was called in by Will Harris, who worked on one of the tugs at the Albert Docks, and asked for his help, as a successful trade union organiser, to unionise the dockers. And, on the Monday morning, as the men were coming to work, Thorne, Harris, and Tom McCarthy, a stevedore, harangued the dockers at the gates, and appealed to them to found a union, and then, in order to secure recognition, to refuse to go to work. This was put to the vote, and the dockers decided to stay out. By midday, the South Docks, Poplar, and Custom House Docks had been organised, the men had agreed not to return to work, and the great dock strike had begun. It had been started not, as was later thought, for the 'dockers' tanner', but as a revolt against the general conditions of work in the docks; it was only afterwards that specific demands were to be formulated. It was Tom Mann who recognised the need for a simple objective, having already come to the conclusion that the Gasworkers had won mainly because they had a one-plank platform. 'Had they gone for half a dozen reforms they might have been agitating vaguely for years without accomplishing anything.' [22] The Gasworkers had their eight-hour day, the Dockers their tanner. Whatever free time Thorne had left over from the needs of his own union, he used to help with the dockers' strike, to assist in setting up the central committee which so successfully ran the operation and to speak at as many meetings as he could. He later recalled this time as one of the most exciting periods of his life.

Just as the Gasworkers had given the original impetus to the dockers, so now the success of the dock strike helped to stimulate further interest in unions amongst all types of labourers, including the Gasworkers. Almost immediately, Thorne found himself with another large strike on his hands, this time in Bristol. The Gasworkers there had initially demanded a rise in wages from the Corporation, which had, at first, been refused and then granted, on the condition that the men should draw five extra retorts a day. This was such an impossible task that they decided to come out on strike. Bristol Corporation, unlike Beckton however, had decided to use blackleg labour, so that the strike, from the very beginning, was bitter and bloody. The police were called in and many of the strikers were prosecuted. But the strike was successful, partly because the strikers were well organised, partly because of the anger aroused throughout the city at the use of blacklegs, and partly simply because gas supplies had run low and the town was threatened with darkness.

The formation of a dockers' union, led by Tillett and Mann,

brought into the open an interesting divergence of views between it and the Gasworkers' Union. Both Mann and Tillett worked against Thorne's principle of 'one man, one ticket, and every man with a ticket', and attempted to put a 'ring fence' round the docks, declaring that a 'closed shop' policy was the only one possible in the industrial situation then prevailing. Thorne always hoped that it would be possible to have one large general union encompassing the needs of all the unskilled labourers, but the ambivalence of his position soon became clear. Because it was impossible to organise such a large union for even the major industries, the concept of 'one man, one ticket' was unrealistic. In practice, it would have meant that the Gasworkers could well have taken over Tillett's Dockers' Union, as they already had a well-established base from which to work. And, indeed, Thorne, himself, when it came to a question of men either joining his union or going to another, always spoke out strongly against those who rejected the Gasworkers.

Will Thorne's links with the SDF and other Socialist groups were of great use in helping to start branches all over the country, and, in one of the most bitter and long drawn out battles that he waged against the employers that year, their help was vital. This strike took place in the India Rubber Works in Silvertown, with the initial demand for a rise from 4¾d to 6d an hour—similar to that of the dockers' tanner—but to be given to the yard labourers. This was agreed to by the owners; the workers then asked for a general increase for all employees. At this, the management balked, and threatened to withdraw the initial increase. The men decided to strike and, as in the case of the dockers, they turned to Will Thorne for support, asking him to organise them. He immediately enrolled them in the Gasworkers' Union, encouraged them to remain on strike, and appealed to his fellow Socialists for support.

Eleanor Marx, fresh from the success of the dockers' strike and already involved with Thorne's Union, threw herself into the battle. For ten weeks, she 'travelled daily to that end-of-the-world place; speaking every day—often twice a day, in all weathers in the open air'.[23] She not only spoke at as many meetings as possible but also formed and then acted as Secretary of the Women's branch of the Gasworkers' Union. She was later elected to the Executive Committee of the Union, to become not only one of the few women to be involved with the early trade union movement, but also one of the few middle class Socialists to be invited to

37

join the Executive Committee of a great union. The strike, however, failed and was the forerunner of an even greater defeat.

For 1889, the great year when 'the spirit of the "New Unionism" was flaming across the country',[24] did not end on a note of triumph for the Union. Now that an eight-hour day had been achieved in many gasworks, Thorne pressed for either the abolition of Sunday work or for the payment of double time. He also argued for a 'closed shop' to strengthen the Union's power. The employers in the London region agreed to his demands for double pay between 6 a.m. and 6 p.m., but not for the hours between 6 and 10 p.m., and, in their turn, suggested a new bonus scheme that would yield 1 per cent on their employees' wages for every penny reduction below 2s 8d per 1,000 cubic feet of gas produced. As a scheme, it had its attraction for the workers, but the employers, particularly the South Metropolitan Gas Company's chairman, Mr Livesey, insisted on an annual contract as a condition for agreeing to withdraw another clause by which strikers forfeited their share of the profits. As the Conspiracy and Protection of Property Act of 1875 had made it a criminal offence for workers to strike without working out the period of their notice, the effect of this was that the union would be forced to give a year's notice of its intentions to strike. As one paper was to say of the scheme— 'It is a sham and a fraud—and we are afraid it is a designed and cruel fraud.'[25] It is clear that Livesey's main objective was to draw the teeth of the Gasworkers' Union.

It was as apparent to Livesey as it was to Thorne that the latter would have no option but to bring his men out. The South Metropolitan chairman had planned carefully for just this contingency. Blacklegs were recruited and housed inside the gasworks so that they need not become involved with pickets. Livesey also persuaded the police to promise all the help they could muster. The actual cause of the strike was the action of three men who agreed to sign the profit sharing contracts, and were expelled from the Union, which then appealed to Livesey to have them dismissed on the grounds that union men should not be made to work with non-unionists. Livesey refused, and the Gasworkers' Union gave notice of strike action.

This time, as Eleanor Marx put it, the Union was 'saved from the "patronage" of the bourgeoisie'.[26] Neither the press nor the police backed the strike, and the Union was out on its own. The blacklegs were immediately put on the job in twelve-hour shifts and so managed to keep up the output. The Union, with 2,000 men out of work, could not keep up the strike payments for long. In February 1890, the Executive began to discuss terms with the employers.

However, Thorne, who was in Plymouth organising new branches, declared in a speech that he 'would not think about giving a day's notice, much less fourteen days' notice', [27] if he had to manage another dispute like that against the South Metropolitan Company. Immediately, Livesey refused to continue with the negotiations and to take back those who had been on strike. It was, declared Thorne, little loss as the men were not in any case anxious to return to work for the South Metropolitan. But the strike had been costly for the Union: £20,000 had been spent in strike pay, and many jobs had been lost. It was clear that, if the employer was able to organise beforehand, the union would normally have much less chance of success.

The London defeat was quickly followed by defeats in Manchester, Salford, and Plymouth. In Leeds, however, where the Council in June 1890 attempted to introduce a four months' notice of strike clause into the contracts, the Gasworkers' Union triumphed. The Corporation had prepared for the strike and organised blacklegs from all over the country. But the Gasworkers were determined not to be beaten. They surrounded the station where the strike breakers were due to appear at three o'clock in the morning, and the police, afraid of possible violence, had to divert the latter to the Town Hall. As more blacklegs arrived, the situation got out of control, fights took place in many parts of the town, and the soldiers were called in. Heavily guarded, the blacklegs were then moved towards the Wortley Gasworks, but, where a railway bridge crossed one of the streets, they were assaulted by a barrage of heavy missiles from above. Many were hurt; and those blacklegs who managed to reach the gasworks clashed with the strikers. By then the strike breakers had had enough. 'When they got inside the works, their main care was not to make gas but to get out of the town as quickly as they possibly could.' [28] The Union paid their fares home. Thorne, who had been summonsed for rioting, had the charge withdrawn by public acclaim, and the Corporation conceded defeat. This was as Thorne wrote later, 'one of the greatest victories both for the union and for the workers who so wholeheartedly supported the strikers.' [29] No wonder that Engels felt that the English proletariat's 'long winter sleep . . . is broken at last. The grandchildren of the Old Chartists are entering the line of battle'. [30] And, to celebrate the victory, he gave his friend a copy of *Capital*, in which he inscribed the words, 'To Will Thorne, the victor of the Leeds battle, with fraternal greetings from Frederick Engels.'[31]

For Thorne, himself, it was a period of intense exertion. He now found himself, at the age of 33, the General Secretary of a growing general union, with no background of education to assist him, and reliant on the help of Eleanor Marx and Will Byford, former secretary of the Yorkshire Glassbottle Association and first Treasurer of the Union, to guide him through the morass of paperwork. His presentation of his first quarterly accounts, with over £30,000 worth of bills and invoices to be tackled, proved a nightmare. The papers, scattered all over the office, were a task that seemed almost insuperable. 'There were bills of every imaginable shape and size, written on all kinds of paper, in pencil and ink, a large proportion of them almost indecipherable. Our office then was just one small room, with meagre and primitive furniture, where the whole of our work had to be done, including the holding of committee meetings.'[32] The disruptive element of constant travel (for Thorne believed in visiting as many new branches as soon as possible) added to the confusion.

Yet Thorne's hard work paid off. By 1892, there were over 70,000 members in the Gasworkers and General Labourers' Union —most, it is true, in the twin occupations of the gasworks and the brick-making factories, but also extending into other industries, such as engineering, jute, the woollen trade, chemicals, and local government. The Union was not as general as Thorne would have wished, but it still covered a fair number of industries.

Despite the growth and appeal of the 'new unions', they still were only a small percentage of the trade union movement. In 1892, only 13 per cent of total trade union membership was in the general unions. And yet, as the 1890 TUC showed, the ideas of the general unions were far more influential than their actual numbers warranted. The previous year, the Gasworkers, having only just been formed, had not been affiliated, and, like other 'new union' General Secretaries, Thorne had been unable to take part in the discussions. A trip to Dundee had, however, coincided with the week of the TUC Congress, and he had been invited to the meetings as a visitor. The battle over whether the eight-hour day should be made legal was raging fiercely, with the delegates, Thorne thought, 'very inconsistent and reactionary'.[33] It was to be quite different the following year. Both the Dockers and the

Gasworkers sent representatives who insistently demanded that the unions should call for a statutory eight-hour day—and saw their appeal succeed. The hold that the old craft unions had had on the TUC had been, if not destroyed, then substantially shaken.

The years of economic boom ended in 1892 and depression followed. The general unions, weakened, to a certain extent, by the vigorous counter-offensive of the employers, were further undermined by the economic recession, and the early promise of a fast growing membership was not realised. How far, if at all, had the original character of Thorne's Gasworkers' Union been modified by its four years of experience?

Beatrice Webb, after interviewing Thorne in 1894 for the Webbs' projected book on trade unionism, gained the impression that the Gasworkers' 'organisation is Socialistic—its objects include the 8-hour day whenever possible, abolition of overtime, same rate of pay for men and women and promotion of legislation in the interest of the workers'.[34] Will Thorne continued to believe that the use of a one-plank platform—first the eight-hour day, then the payment for overtime—was the most effective way of achieving results. The eight-hour day was, however, the most important objective for Thorne. For, as he wrote in 1892 he believed that it was the most 'immediate method of meeting the problem of the unemployed',[35] because it removed competition from the labour market.

He linked the eight-hour movement to his Socialist principles. Time and time again he urged his members not to forget that 'as long as capital rules the Imperial and Local Government machinery of this and other countries, so long will they, the workers, have their noses kept to the grindstone'.[36] He also made it clear that it was useless to make any distinction between the two political parties, for, from a 'labour standpoint they are one and the same'.[37] Thorne, throughout his quarterly reports, continued to exhort his members to remember their true foes, the capitalists, and never to forget that during 'a strike there are no Tories or Liberals amongst the strikers, they are all workers. At Election times there are no workers, only Liberals and Tories. During an election there are Tory and Liberal Capitalists, and all of them are friends of the workers. . . . They are all capitalists and enemies of the workers.'[38] And, in 1894, as in 1889, Thorne urged union members to become involved in politics.

41

Thorne did more than exhort; he became personally involved with International Socialism—obviously under the influence of the Avelings and their friends. He represented the Union at the 1891 Brussels International Congress (see Chapter 4), and helped to prepare a long report of the labour movement in Britain. The Executive Committee of the Gasworkers wrote an open letter to all working men's organisations, which was read out at the Brussels Congress, suggesting that each country should set up an International Labour Secretary to prevent the introduction of unfair labour from one country to another, that is, 'of workers, who not knowing the conditions of the labour struggle in a particular country, are imported into that country by the capitalists, in order to reduce wages, lengthen the hours of labour, or both'.[39] He saw the war against the employers not only in the immediate field of the shop floor but in the wider one of the international labour movement.

By 1892, Thorne and his Union were still militant. It should, however, be remembered that Thorne never believed in indiscriminate militancy. From the start, he thought that strikes should be properly planned and organised, under the guidance of the Executive, so that union resources need not be wasted in a hopeless cause—though there were occasions, as in the Manchester and Salford strikes, when, although he knew the Union was fighting a losing battle, he was forced, for the sake of the Union's prestige, to support precipitate action by local branches. It was typical of Thorne's realistic attitude that, as the boom began to recede, he counselled restraint. He thought that, as the country was 'entering one of those Periodical Depressions in trade with which we workers are so well acquainted, we should therefore be very judicious in all our movements in treating with the employer on matters connected with work and wages, and, whenever possible without loss of dignity and self-respect, all disputes should be settled in the most quiet and expedient manner, especially during a time of depression'.[40] This did not mean that Thorne had abandoned militancy, but he felt that it was his duty, in a difficult period, to preserve union strength. But, if restraint was to be the strategy for the time being, Thorne held out hope for the future. Though stressing the power of the employers, he urged his members not to feel dismay. The time would come when the workers would wring from the capitalists 'the machinery of Parliamentary and municipal government, and use it for the protection of those concessions which they have gained through the respective organisations'.[41] His members were not to forget that they were not only union men but workers in a capitalist society whose objective it was to gain their political as well as economic rights.

As the new revised rules of the Gasworkers and General Labourers, written in 1892, declared, the working class ought to put its fate into the hands of the trade unions, which were the coming champions of the class struggle and which would so unite the working class that it would march 'steadily and irresistibly forward to its ultimate goal—the Emancipation of the Working Class.'

Chapter 4

'New' Politics

The years from 1894 to 1910 were, on the whole, barren industrially; and the main achievements of Thorne and his Union were political.

By 1894, the recession, of which Thorne had warned his members, had arrived. Although the economy recovered at the time of the Boer War, the subsequent years till 1910 were mostly years of uncertain growth and periodic high unemployment, which affected the new unions, in particular. The membership trends of the Gasworkers fluctuated but did not show any overall growth. In 1890, the Gasworkers numbered 60,000; in 1896 the membership had fallen to the all time low of 24,000; in 1900, following the pick up of the economy, there were 48,000 members; by 1910 the membership had dropped back again to 32,000.

These were also years, in which many employers, worried by foreign competition and falling profits and frightened by the apparent strength of the trade unions, pursued a tough, anti-union line. They also attemped to use the courts against them.

Thorne's reaction to this new and obviously dangerous situation for his Union was to diversify both industrially and geographically. During the 1890s, the Gasworkers built up their membership, particularly in the Birmingham and London districts, amongst building labourers. In 1899, Thorne claimed that the Union had 13,650 members in the building industry. The Gasworkers also recruited shipyard workers in the North-East, tinplate workers in South Wales, iron and steel and colliery surface workers in Yorkshire and Nottingham, metal workers in Birmingham, and dyers and engineering workers in Lancashire. Thorne's aim that the Gasworkers should include everyone 'from the gravedigger to the diamond cutter . . . from the pit driver to the washerman'[1] may have been fanciful, but the Gasworkers had to be 'general' to survive. Even so, the Union continued to rely on its relatively solid base in the gas industry and tried to extend into other areas of secure employment, particularly in local government.

The Union's strength also shifted geographically. During these years, Thorne opened up new districts in Lancashire, the North, in South Wales, and for a short period, in Scotland. In 1892, the London district had included over half the Union's members; by the end of 1910, London had only a tenth of the membership, and Lancashire, Leeds, and the Northern districts were all larger.

Thorne was well aware from his own success that, in union organisation, outstanding personalities were as important as any factor. He, therefore, chose district secretaries who were not only competent organisers but who also had minds of their own. His wooing of J. R. Clynes, the future President of the Union and Cabinet Minister, is typical of Thorne's approach. Clynes had already, in 1892, been asked to help form a branch of the Gas-workers' Union in Oldham; he was holding a large recruitment meeting there when Will Thorne approached the crowd which to his wonder 'was gathered about a mere slip of a lad, hardly more than a boy. Having come to be amused I remained to be amazed. After three quarters of an hour's dissertation from this stripling, I decided that he knew as much about Lancashire's industrial troubles as I did myself,' [2] and promptly offered Clynes the job of district organiser for that region.

As other districts developed, pressure grew to change the basis of the Union's government. At the start, the Gasworkers had been run from the London office and its governing body was drawn from the London district only; the new districts had considerable local autonomy but no central representation. In 1900, the weekly meeting of the Executive was supplemented by quarterly meetings of the General Executive Council, made up of London members together with other district representatives, who tended to be the district secretaries. The new system, however, was still considered insufficiently representative. It was, therefore, agreed, at the 1908 Biennial Congress, that a General Council should be set up, consisting of the General Secretary and two representatives from each district, one the district secretary and the other a 'lay' member, i.e. not a permanent paid official, chosen by the district. In this way, it was hoped to involve the membership more fully in the running of the Union.

During this period, Thorne's attitude to militant action became more pragmatic. In the years of depression, he counselled caution.

In 1894, he exhorted his members to rely on the advice of their officials, declaring that 'a firm stand should be made against men coming out on strike, unless oppressed to such an extent that their position is unbearable'.[3] Again, be 'careful,' he warned in 1900, as the Boer War boom petered out, 'of rushing into any dispute as there are signs of trade in many parts of the country being on the downward grade, but where there is a good prospect of success in improving the members' position, then by all means do so'.[4] Indeed, whenever he saw the opportunity, he pressed his members' case to the limit. For example, during the boom, Thorne used the Gasworkers' strength to advance the claims of his building workers throughout the Midlands and the South. By 1900, the Union had secured wage increases in about forty towns. In a ballot that year of the Union's building workers' membership in London, there was an overwhelming majority for a strike. But the rest of the building labourers' unions, without the resources of other workers behind them, thwarted the Gasworkers' strategy by refusing to back the strike. What Thorne wished to avoid was the expenditure of union resources on lost causes—as in 1902, when South Wales tinplate workers struck in vain for a reduction of hours and when there were fruitless strikes amongst London brickworkers, Barnsley surface workers, Lancashire printers' labourers and Grimsby fish dockers.

When Thorne and his district secretaries were able to secure recognition from an employer, they tried to reach agreement on wages and conditions. The Union reports show some wage increases during the boom years. Even in 1897, before the boom had gathered strength, Clynes wrote that the Lancashire district had gained advances in 'wages and improved conditions . . . for telephone workers in five different towns, and we have to record further gains for Gasworkers and Corporation workers in Blackburn and Stockport'.[5] In exchange for 'closed' shop arrangements and favourable wages and conditions, the Gasworkers even went so far as to make a 'compact' with both the Birmingham metal trades and the Yorkshire Piece Dyers Association to come out on strike against any firm that sold at prices below those laid down by the employers' association. Thorne was not happy about these last agreements; when the Birmingham Alliance fell through in 1902, he was delighted for, as he wrote to his members, 'We have never been favourable to the formation of an alliance with the employers, because we believe it is against the true principles of Trade Unions. . . . This talk of harmony between capital and labour reminds one of the prophecy about the lion laying down with the lamb inside.' [6] In any case, the problem with collective bargaining in the early 1900s, as with militant action, was that it was conducted against the background of an uncertain economic climate; the employers were more anxious to negotiate cuts rather than to agree to rises in wages. The result, as with unsuccessful strikes, was disillusionment and a falling away in membership.

As is usual in times of recession, unions fought for each others' members. In 1901, the new Workers' Union introduced funeral benefits and an optional sickness benefit. To meet this competition, Thorne was forced to modify his earlier 'no benefits' policy. In 1904, the General Secretary pointed out 'this union has always been recognised as a fighting union, as we believe in getting more material advantages than merely being a rate-saving institution, but I still cannot close my eyes . . . to this keen competition.' [7] A permanent Disablement Fund was, therefore, set up with a maximum payment of £50 for total permanent disablement and £25 for partial disablement. To pay for this new benefit, the weekly contribution was raised from 2½d to 3d.

Legal judgements created a situation whereby trades unionists might be sued on grounds of conspiracy: even worse, the Taff Vale case of 1901 made trade union funds liable. Thorne warned that in 'consequence of the recent decisions which have been given against Trade Unions all workmen should be exceedingly careful before they attempt to come out on strike'.[8] In 1903, the Gasworkers' Executive told its districts that they must order back to work all strikers coming out without the Executive's authority.

The pessimism of those years was reflected in Pete Curran's Presidential address to the 1904 Biennial Congress. He summarised the reasons why he thought the Union had failed to expand. It was partly, he said, due to the trade depression, and partly to the introduction of labour-saving machinery; while such decisions as the Taff Vale judgement, coupled with other legal cases, made the job of the trades unions that much more difficult. Four years later, Curran was still gloomy. 'Membership,' he told the 1908 Biennial Congress, changed because the union catered 'for what is called the great fluctuating mass of unskilled workmen',[9] who never settled down, and had never been trained for any special industry. He again stressed, as he had in 1904, the effect that labour-saving machinery had on the unskilled labourers, who were always the first to lose their jobs. But he ended on a more hopeful note; the Gasworkers' Union, in spite of the many vicissitudes that had beset it remained the 'most influential organisation of general labourers in the United Kingdom'.[10]

The difficult years of the late 1890s and early 1900s more than ever convinced Thorne of the need for political action to supplement and strengthen the industrial activities of trade unions. At both local and national level, Thorne believed, the workers needed to create their own political organisation to fight for working-class interests. Thorne and his Union were deeply involved in the events that led up to the formation of the Labour Representation Committee in 1900 and the emergence of the Labour Party at the General Election of 1906 as a sizeable political force. At local government level, the Gasworkers were in the vanguard of a movement to elect Labour councillors—and, in 1898, Thorne himself played a leading role in the first Labour-controlled council ever elected.

Thorne's belief in the necessity for independent political action by the workers was partly the consequence of his Socialist views and partly the result of his trade union experience. But, for a full understanding of Thorne's political commitment, his links with International Socialism must also be considered. It was the Avelings who involved Thorne in the work of the Second International. The First International, founded in 1864 by Karl Marx, had broken up in sterile squabbling between Marxists and Anarchists; the Second International, which was set up in Paris in 1889, was far more important. It became a forum at which the young but growing European Socialist parties could thrash out the great problems of the day; whether a Socialist party should gain power by revolution or by Parliamentary means; how Socialists could prevent wars. The International passed resolutions on all these, and, when it was a question that concerned party discipline or the correct interpretation of Marxist doctrine, the member parties were expected to obey.

The Paris Second International Congress of 1889 resolved to call for May Day celebrations to be held wherever possible, as a sign of solidarity among the working classes. In 1890 the Avelings, who were concerned in the organisation of the British end of the demonstrations, persuaded Thorne to participate both by arranging for his union to march from Canning Town and by speaking on one of the platforms set up in Hyde Park for the occasion.

Thorne was the Gasworkers' delegate at the Brussels Congress of 1891 where his union played an important part. At that Congress, the Gasworkers, together with the Legal Eight Hours and International Labour League, the Bloomsbury Socialist Society and the Battersea Labour League issued a 'Report' on the labour movement in Britain. Based on a series of studies of the labour scene, it was widely acclaimed by delegates as one of the most valuable contributions made to the Conference, and was translated into many languages. Certainly, there was much truth in Thorne's declaration that 'Our Union is at the head of the advanced movement.' [11]

The Brussels Congress was followed by another Congress, held at Zurich in 1893. Thorne attended as a TUC delegate (the TUC having been persuaded to send representatives), while the Avelings represented the Gasworkers. George Bernard Shaw, who also went to Zurich, gives a memorable picture of Thorne. The weather was very hot and Thorne tried to cool down by immersing himself in Lake Zurich where he 'swam like a centaur, breast high out of the water, to the admiration of all spectators and the envy of all sculptors'.[12] At Zurich, it was decided that London should be the next venue for the Congress to be held in 1896. Thorne was one of the chief organisers of that Congress. He was a member of the preliminary arrangements committee, Chairman of the fund raising committee, and the Secretary of the Committee that ran the Conference. He also attended the Paris Congress of 1900, the Amsterdam Congress of 1904, the Stuttgart Congress of 1907, and the Copenhagen Congress of 1910.

Thorne's participation in International Socialism was important to him for a number of reasons. He enjoyed visiting other countries (he went to concerts and drank light lager in Belgium, learnt about Swiss compulsory military service, was worried by German militarism, and was impressed by the neatness of the Danes). He was stimulated by meeting the well-known leaders and thinkers of Socialism, like Jaurés, Bebel, Liebknecht, and Bernstein, and by listening to the great debates of the Second International. Perhaps most important of all, the growing electoral success of the independent Socialist parties in Germany, Austria, Sweden, Belgium, and, to a lesser extent, in France underlined for him the need for the formation of a real workers' party at all levels in Britain.

The Gasworkers had a deliberate policy of putting up candidates in local elections. By 1893, eighteen men and women had been elected to local government bodies. This was, in part, an attempt to influence local authorities in favour of trade unionism in services such as gas and water. More fundamentally, Thorne felt that the challenge to the capitalist classes must be made at local as well as national level.

In 1891, Thorne, himself, stood as a Socialist candidate for the borough of West Ham and was the first member of the SDF to be successful in local elections. As his Union had its headquarters in West Ham and he himself lived there, it was natural that he should become involved in local politics. There was much to be done. West Ham 'that great city of the poor, lying like a flat unlovely wilderness of mean streets',[13] had only recently received its charter and its services were scanty and ill organised. The Borough's main industries, such as gasworks, engineering and shipbuilding were all affected by recessions; and, as a result, most of the Borough's workers were frequently unemployed. But the burden of providing relief (which, under the Poor Law Act of 1834, was a local responsibility) fell, in West Ham, which was outside the new LCC, on a small middle-class, who objected strongly to any efforts made to increase assistance to the unemployed. In addition, the housing situation was appalling; there were many slums and severe cases of overcrowding. Not nearly enough schools had been built and there were scarcely any social amenities of any kind. To a committed Socialist like Thorne, it was his duty to try and improve the conditions of his own borough.

Thorne's arrival on the Council in 1891, after a campaign which was both heated and bitter, was greeted with enthusiasm, at least by the local press, which managed at one and the same time to compliment the new councillor and attack his party. 'Thorne,' wrote one editor, 'is one of the most earnest, straightforward, reliable common sense men, in the Labour movement. He is that, alas, rare exception in Labour movements—a man whom the workers love and are proud of, a man who never backbites another, and a man who works solely for the movement and has absolutely no personal aims.'[14] Will Thorne's reputation had preceded him.

His election platform, which had included such revolutionary concepts as the building of public baths and wash houses for the borough, municipalisation of the tram service, and the eight-hour day, should have warned Thorne's fellow councillors that he would not be prepared to accept a passive role. Immediately he he was elected, he set out, as a Socialist and trade unionist, to question the assumptions of the West Ham Borough Council. As a symbol of his commitment to Socialism, he willingly signed a declaration binding him to the Federation. In it, he pledged 'to work for the objects in the programme of the SDF if elected to the Town Council for the Borough of West Ham, and also to submit to the guidance of the Canning Town Branch on all questions concerning my actions and votes on the Town Council, and I further pledge myself to withdraw from the Town Council if requested to do so by a special meeting of the Branch and Branches summoned according to rule.' [15]

Within two months, he had started agitating for trade union wages to be paid by all contractors employed by the Borough, as well as demanding that all municipal employees should be given an eight-hour day and a minimum wage. And as unemployment grew, so Will Thorne became more vociferous, insisting that the unemployed should be given, not charity (in the form of outdoor relief), but work.

In 1894, the situation in West Ham had become acute. A proposition from one of the local industrialists, Mr H. F. Hills, to hand over, on certain conditions, £1,000 to the West Ham unemployment fund was, therefore, snatched at eagerly by the Council. Hills stipulated that the Borough was to employ workmen at 4d rather than the current rate of 6d an hour and that they were to be given work for only six hours a day and four days a week—to differentiate, so he argued, between the competent and the incompetent workman. Thorne's angry protests at these conditions were drowned by the majority of the councillors, anxious not to have to increase the rate demand.

If his fellow councillors hoped that they had succeeded in silencing Thorne, they were soon disillusioned; he had no intention of being defeated on a basic trade union principle. With great speed, he organised the SDF, the ILP, the Trades Council, and all local branches of trades unions in the area, to march on the Council at its next sitting, and occupy the public gallery. He himself remained in the Council Chamber, and it was Pete Curran, one of the organisers of the Gasworkers and later MP for Jarrow, who led the delegation. Curran, carrying the red flag of the Federation on high, demanded, on behalf of the unemployed, that trade union rates and conditions should be applied to all relief work in the Borough. It was a moment of high drama, as the crowds surged, the public galleries heaved with excitement, and, for the first time in British history, the red flag of Socialism was waved triumphantly in such an 'austere and dignified place' [16] as a Council Chamber. The West Ham councillors bowed to public pressure.

It was a feat of which Will Thorne was justly proud and which made his name famous throughout the Borough. However, four years later, the exploits of the West Ham Socialists made a national impact. Following Thorne's election, the number of Labour councillors grew. By 1898, Thorne had been joined on the Council by other members of his Union, notably Arthur Hayday and Jack Jones, both of whom later became Members of Parliament. Following the elections of November 1898, the 'Labour Group' gained a slender majority. For the first time, a Labour-controlled council had been elected. Thorne was jubilant. 'We hold West Ham in the palm of our hands',[17] he triumphantly told a local press man. The occasion was indeed historic: 'For the first time in English history the Labour Party has acquired absolute command of a Town Council, and the municipality which it rules is a great one. The opportunity is not only immense, but unique. The Labour Party as a whole will be judged by what it does in West Ham. All over the kingdom the eyes of observers will be upon it.' [18]

How was Labour's electoral success achieved? First, the Group had been able to present a united front. In fact the 'Labour Group' was more of a coalition than a unified party; it was composed of not only the Labour, but also the Radical, Progressive, Irish Nationalist, and Trade Union vote. Secondly, the group benefited from the well-publicised campaigns that had been waged in the Borough by such famous personalities as Keir Hardie (who had been MP for West Ham) and Will Thorne, who, both through his union activities and his fights within the Council Chamber, had earned much respect for himself. There is no doubt also that the engineering lockout of 1897 helped to awaken trade union voters (especially as the Engineers put up two candidates) from their general apathy. Finally (and perhaps most important of all) the 'Labour Group' ran on a clear and constructive programme—the eight-hour day, better housing, payment of trade union rates, and, something that appealed to many electors, the municipalisation of the tramways. It was this specific programme, in contrast to the personalised and over-confident nature of the opposition's approach, which gained the support of the voters of West Ham.

The press, in particular *The Times*, watched avidly for the first mistakes of the new Council. In fact, success for the Group was short-lived. The Group only had a majority of one in the Chamber and its efforts to implement its election programme were bitterly attacked both within the Council Chamber by the opposition and outside by the press. Council meetings were marred by fierce invective on both sides. The Group was criticised for signing, as Thorne had previously, a declaration by which they agreed to abide by the majority vote. To Thorne, it was the only way to keep the various interests united. If it was, as a 'Labour Group' manifesto declared, 'the boldest attempt ever made in the world's history to win a brighter and nobler day for the toilers', it could only be implemented by a determined and united common front. However, to their opponents, the discipline of the Group—something new in local politics—smacked of revolutionary tactics, and was vigorously denounced.

Thorne and his fellow councillors were always conscious of the need for the utmost speed in the implementation of their policies. They could not forget that there was 'no other town of the size of West Ham in the kingdom where schools, hospitals, town halls, and other buildings have all had to be provided in so short a space of time'.[19] In December 1898, they took over part of the North Metropolitan Tramways Co. They also introduced policies to tackle the housing shortage and high rents. They started to buy land on which to build houses. Finding it difficult to get enough land by private treaty, the Council adopted the revolutionary proposal that compulsory purchase orders should be obtained through a Parliamentary Bill, which would enable the Borough to buy about a hundred acres of different sites. However, this suggested Bill was the following year put to the poll, and resulted in a defeat for the 'Labour Group'—though if there had been a one man, one vote, franchise instead of a plural voting system (related to property) the 'Labour Group' would have had a majority of 2,409.[20] In addition, a fever hospital extension and a Borough lunatic asylum were built—by a new works department set up by the Council, the first ever in the country. The Council's employees were given the eight-hour day or forty-eight hours a week; Labour Day, 1 May, became a paid holiday, and a minimum wage of 30s a week was established. For the borough's unemployed, a register was opened and the men set to planting trees. Free concerts and open libraries on Sundays were among the other innovations pushed through.

Thorne, throughout, tried to enlist support for the Council from working men. Holding open-air meetings throughout the Borough, he emphasised time and time again that the working classes could only get emancipation through the political system and not through their trade unions alone. In defending the controversial decision only to employ union men on Council work he said that 'the ordinary working man has no freedom. He has simply to take the wages which are offered him and submit to all the employer's conditions, or walk the streets. I believe in a certain amount of coercion on the part of workmen to make men join the unions because, if no trades unions existed, the conditions of employment would be worse than they are now.' [21] To Thorne, his role as a councillor was both an extention of his fight for trade unionism and for a better society for the workers.

However, Thorne's efforts to sustain the 'Labour Group' in power were in vain. In the elections of 1900, they were defeated by an opposition, united in their determination to return to office. The cry of 'high rates' and 'extravagant spending' in addition to the adverse publicity that had dogged the 'Labour Group' throughout their term of office ensured the success of what, as one paper later described them, was 'a curious amalgamation of publicans and sinners; Liberals and Tories; pot-house politicians and teetotallers'.[22] The 'Labour Group' remained in opposition until 1910. Thorne, himself, was to remain on the Council for over forty years.

However, though the 'Labour Group' failed to get their full programme implemented and many of their projects were abandoned, their reforms (such as compulsory purchase orders, local authority housing, municipally owned transport, direct labour departments, trade union rates and conditions) foreshadowed many of the achievements of twentieth-century local government. In this field, as in others, Thorne was an innovator. As Harold Laski, in a tribute to Will Thorne, wrote, 'The mean streets of West Ham are less mean because he lived there'.[23]

Throughout the 1890s, Thorne argued the case for an independent and Socialist Labour Party at national level. There was some talk, he wrote, in 1897, at the time of the engineering lockout, that trades unions should not meddle in politics. 'This cry is a foolish one. Do not employers use all their political power to make laws to keep the worker's nose to the grindstone? What have we, the wage earners, to lose by using our political power? Only our chains.' All within the Union must therefore, 'use the political weapon with a view to breaking down a system which forces them and their class to be used not as human beings, but as profit making machines.'[24]

The general climate of opinion within the trade unions was, in fact, beginning to move towards the ideas of Thorne and other Socialist leaders. Perhaps the most important factor was the growing counter-offensive of the employers, launched both industrially and through the courts against the unions. One of their most decisive moves was that made by the Engineering Employers' Federation who organised a lockout in 1897 against the craft unions' attempt to force the employers to agree that machines which replaced old skills should still be operated by craftsmen. The result was largely a defeat for the trade unions. And the 1899 judgement of the Court of Appeal, in the case of *Lyons* v. *Wilkins*, which appeared to remove trades union picketing rights, convinced many trade union leaders that the law now backed the employers.

These anti-union moves strengthened the arguments of the Socialist groups which increased their influence amongst the trade unions during the 1890s. In 1893, the Independent Labour Party was founded at Bradford, in order to send working men to Parliament, independent of the Tory and Liberal parties. Unlike the SDF, it managed to capture the support of the younger trade unionists; amongst the Gasworkers, both Clynes and Pete Curran, who was a founder member, joined the ILP. Thorne was approached by Keir Hardie at the TUC Congress of 1892 to help promote the new party, but, though he supported its objectives, he told Hardie that he intended to remain a member of the SDF.

At the Plymouth Congress of 1899, the 'new' unions and the Socialists won the day. By a narrow majority, Congress passed the following resolution: 'This Congress, having regard to its decisions in former years, and with a view to securing a better representation of the interests of Labour in the House of Commons, hereby instructs the Parliamentary Committee to invite the cooperation of all the Co-operative, Socialists, Trade Unions, and other working organisations to jointly co-operate on lines mutually agreed upon, in convening a special congress of representatives from such of the above mentioned organisations as may be willing to take part, to devise ways and means for securing the return of an increased number of Labour members to the next Parliament'[25]

As the terms of the resolution indicate, it was not a vote for

Socialism, but it was a vote for ensuring more effective Labour representation.

A preliminary committee was set up to discuss the agenda for the coming conference and first met on 5 December, 1899. It consisted of representatives of the trade unions, of the ILP, who were represented by Keir Hardie and Ramsay MacDonald, of the SDF, and of the Fabian Society. Thorne, who had been elected to the Parliamentary Committee in 1894, represented the TUC. The work of this preliminary committee was crucial. It drew up the agenda for the conference and proposed a series of resolutions. The main problem for the committee was to devise a formula that would not antagonise the trade unions, the majority of whom had no commitment to Socialism. Although MacDonald was the dominating influence, Thorne's own role as a link between the Socialists and the trade unions was also vital.

The Conference, which met on 27 February, 1900 at the Memorial Hall in London, accomplished what few had previously thought possible. Trade unionists and Socialists agreed to run candidates under the same umbrella and to form an autonomous Labour group in Parliament. And, although it was more of a federation of interest than a united party, a major step had been taken towards the formation of an independent Labour Party.

The Gasworkers played a key role in the development of the Labour Representation Committee (LRC). The major unions (the miners, the engineers, textile workers, and carpenters) did not join at once; and the Gasworkers' Union, after the Railway Servants, was the second largest union to affiliate. The Union was represented on the Executive of the new body by Pete Curran, who in 1904 was joined by Clynes. Thorne, himself became involved in national politics from early on, and stood as Parliamentary candidate for West Ham South in the General Election of 1900.

The background to his candidature was somewhat complicated. Keir Hardie had stood for West Ham in 1892 and had been elected. He was, however, defeated in 1895. The question of his candidature was raised soon after, partly because he had previously won the seat through the help of the Gasworkers (and Thorne himself was now interested in national politics), and partly because the SDF was stronger in the constituency than the ILP. Events went in Thorne's favour. By 1900, he had become the best-known figure in the area, with powerful trade union and local authority connections. Hardie, having previously stated that had he won in 1895 he would have stood down for Thorne at the next election, agreed, somewhat reluctantly, to look for another seat. It was Thorne, therefore, who stood for West Ham South in 1900.

The 1900 election, coming as it did so soon after the Labour Representation Committee had been set up, found the new Labour organisation without much central direction. Thorne, himself, stood as a Labour and Socialist candidate on a programme that included the introduction of the legal eight-hour day, the nationalisation of the means of production and transport, improved factory legislation and the setting up of state pension schemes. It was a political manifesto that owed much to the influence of the SDF. Rather surprisingly, Thorne was defeated. The explanation of the SDF was that the organisation was poor, that old registers were used and that there was hardly any canvassing done at all.

Only two LRC candidates were elected at the 1900 election, which was an overwhelming triumph for the Conservative government. However, the Taff Vale judgement of 1901 appeared to put all trade union activities at risk. The major trade unions, except the miners, drew the appropriate conclusion and joined the LRC. Thorne urged his members to support the new party and working-class politics.

It was, he told his members in 1903, no use becoming involved in 'the fiscal ferment' of the tariff controversy; too easy to 'neglect the substance of their own welfare for the shadow of Free Trade or the mirage of Protection'; either way the Tories and the Liberals were little interested in the needs of the working classes. What was important was to achieve powerful 'unions, together with a strong working-class political party in the House of Commons' which would enable the workers to gain higher wages and shorter hours 'in spite of the employing classes'.[26] At the end of that quarterly report, Thorne printed the manifestos both of the Labour Representation Committee and the SDF.

Meanwhile, Thorne was having difficulties in his constituency, mainly because of his membership of the SDF. The SDF, which had been given two seats on the Executive of the new body, withdrew from the LRC in 1901 because it was not Socialist enough. In 1903, Jack Jones, a member of the Gasworkers, and also of the SDF, narrowly failed to commit the LRC conference to the 'public ownership of the means of production, distribution and exchange'; Thorne also thought that the time had come when the unions ought to support a Socialist and Labour Party of their own. At West Ham he decided to run, as he had in 1900, as a 'Socialist and

Labour' candidate. The LRC, which had been too weak to im pose its will in 1900, now refused to allow him to do so. A row ensued: Thorne declared that he would stand down, as his own West Ham party, which had a majority of SDF members, wanted him to stand as a Socialist candidate. Clynes, always adept in difficult situations, attempted to save this one. A resolution was passed at 'the Gasworkers' Biennial Congress in 1904, strongly requesting 'the various representatives promoting Will Thorne's candidature in South West Ham to assent to his running under the common title imposed on all candidates supported by the LRC'.[27] As Thorne's local party was made up largely of members of the Gasworkers, Clynes thought that they would be amenable to a union directive. However, a special joint delegate meeting representing the trade unions, ILP and SDF in South West Ham, declared that they would conduct the election in their own way. Thorne agreed to this decision for, as he reported to his own union members, 'I cannot very well see my way clear to overthrow the decision of about eighty *bona-fide* workmen, who are prepared to pull off their coats and do everything that lays in their power to secure my return.'[28] An impasse appeared to have been reached. However, once more the Union intervened, and this time was successful in persuading the local party to allow Thorne to stand as a Labour candidate.

Had the Union not won the day, Thorne might have had difficulties in winning the seat. The secret pact that MacDonald made with the Liberals in 1903, by which most LRC candidates did not have to face Liberal opposition, meant that the LRC ticket became much more valuable. In the end, Thorne had a straight fight and received strong 'non-conformist' support—a slightly unlikely occurrence for a protégé of Eleanor Marx. Though running as a LRC candidate, Thorne issued an un-ashamedly Socialist manifesto. The electors of West Ham South were exhorted that a vote for Thorne 'is a vote on behalf of the down trodden and oppressed, a vote on behalf of the famished children in our schools, and of the disinherited in our pauper bastilles; it is a word of hope to the struggling masses in all parts of Great Britain, and of encouragement to all who suffer under the heel of Capitalism; a blow struck for the workers in that war between Capitalism and Labour which must be waged relentlessly until the emancipation of the workers is achieved by the abolition of the Capitalist system'. And the Countess of Warwick, arriving in a red motor car to help in the election, told the electors of West

Ham that 'they had a man in Mr Will Thorne who was the envy of the constituency'.[29] The voters responded and Thorne was returned to Parliament with a majority over his Conservative opponent of 5,237. It was the start of a Parliamentary career that was to last till 1945.

The 1906 election was a great victory for the Liberals, who had an overall majority of 84. But the emergence of the Labour Party (as it now called itself) created a sensation too, with Balfour, the Conservative leader, suggesting that the new Liberal Prime Minister was now a mere cork on the Socialist tide. Out of the twenty-nine LRC candidates returned, only Will Thorne was a sponsored member of the Gasworkers. However, Clynes was also elected for Manchester North-East, as was Parker, another member of the Gasworkers, for Halifax. When Pete Curran was elected for Jarrow at a 1907 by-election, the Gasworkers became the second largest trade union group in the House of Commons— and the largest affiliated to the Labour Party (as the miners did not join until 1909).

Fittingly, Thorne's maiden speech in May 1906, was on unemployment. In it, he spoke up for the unemployed of West Ham. Though there is a convention that maiden speeches are non-controversial, Thorne was unable to check his passionate concern for the plight of the unemployed. He said that he was willing 'if the government did not do anything, to advise the unemployed . . . to go and help themselves'.[30] Stirring words indeed! In fact, Thorne had had stage fright just before he began to speak. 'I felt,' he wrote later, 'as though I was chloroformed. Every eye in the House seemed to be fixed upon me. I imagined that everyone's ears were three or four times their normal size and that all were reaching out to catch the words I felt I could never get out of my mouth.'[31]

A year later he again brought up the subject of unemployment, pointing out that there was no legislation in the offing and suggesting that the Liberals ought not only to introduce an eight-hour Bill but should bring forward a Bill 'so as to have at hand some machinery by which when a man dropped out of employment he could be picked out at once, because in most cases when men were out of work for a week they were, vulgarly speaking, on their beams ends and had to pawn something to find food for their wives, and children'.[32] He spoke with the voice of experience, for West Ham had, in 1905, gone through the worst unemployment year within living memory.

By no stroke of the imagination could Thorne be called a conventional Member of Parliament. Though a great user of Question Time, he was not a parliamentary orator. When speaking, he resembled, as a journalist once remarked, 'a boy's clockwork engine fitted with a good spring wound to capacity and then released before the engine is placed on the rails. The wheels dash round at amazing speed and stop when the spring has run down'.[33] He was also given to interruptions and loud exclamations, and even to whistle-blowing. At times, he expressed himself in unparliamentary language. One of the best examples of this was in 1909 over the coming state visit of Tsar Nicholas II of Russia to Britain. Thorne put down a question asking if the visit were to be official, and, on the Foreign Secretary's admission that it was, the following exchange took place: '*Mr W. Thorne:* I hope he will get his deserts when he gets here. The British do not want him. *Major Anstruther-Gray:* May I, Sir, call attention to the fact that an Hon. Member said that when the Tsar of Russia came here he would get his deserts? Is that in order? *Mr W. Thorne:* I said I hope he would ... He is an inhuman beast.'[34]

An equally controversial exchange, of which Thorne was rather proud, took place during the committee stage of the Finance Bill on 14 July 1909. The debate was heated and Thorne, sitting next to the Labour MP for Gorton, John Hodge, who was continuously interrupting, suggested to Hodge that 'he had better shut up, for there's going to be trouble'. No sooner said than Thorne, himself, was accused by a Conservative MP of being in no fit state to take part in the debate. This was too much for the MP for West Ham, who springing to his feet, shouted 'I am as sober as you are, my young friend'.[35] Immediately there were cries of 'withdraw'; and Lord Winterton, who had made the remark, did so grudgingly. Thorne accused him of being a liar, and refused to take back his remark unless the Tory was prepared to withdraw properly. Whereupon Thorne was asked to leave the Chamber by the Chairman for using unparliamentary language. It was Thorne who had the last word; for the episode had a curious sequel. Most Members agreed that Thorne had been slandered by Winterton, and the Prime Minister, Asquith, therefore asked that the entry of the suspension in the House Journal should be expunged from the Minutes, making this only the third time that the records had thus been erased.

If Thorne appeared controversial to his opponents, he also

managed, at times, to have the same effect on members of his own party. One occasion on which they were aroused, in particular the ILP members, was his introduction of the Citizen's Army Bill in 1908. The SDF, under the guidance of Hyndman, believed, in view of the unsettled state of Europe, that expenditure on defence was a justifiable outlay of public funds. They also considered that, the sooner all citizens were trained in the use of arms, the quicker their goal of Socialism would be reached. For only when the workers were armed would there be 'a guarantee of individual liberty, of social freedom and of national independence'.[36] Thorne's Bill was in answer to the government's Territorial and Reserve Forces Act, setting up volunteer units in association with, and supplementary to, the Regular Army, which was seen by the SDF as a form of conscription. The Bill's main provisions were that every male between the ages of 18 and 29 would have annual military training in camps, and then pass into the reserves. The citizen soldiers would elect their officers and have full democratic control over them; they were not to be called out to act in any case of civil disturbance or to be mobilised in any emergency other than an actual or threatened invasion. The authority for enforcing and administering the Act would be the city or borough council of each district. Such a revolutionary concept naturally had no support from the government. The ILP, however, were even more vicious in their attack on the Bill, announcing that it was only because the air was full of war-mongering rumours that Thorne had the audacity to 'unbag his little abortion to the public gaze'. His manner 'shows that he rightly appreciates the ungainly character of the nursling committed to his charge'.[37] The Bill made no progress.

In the period before the war, though the Gasworkers played a part in shaping some of the reforms passed by the Liberal government, Thorne was often impatient with the progress being made by the Labour Party in Parliament. In part, it was the frustration of being a member of a small group which was, by force of circumstances, dependent on the Liberals for any success with Parliamentary legislation. Thorne's own Bills on the Minimum Wage and the Nationalisation of the Railways did not get far. In part, also, it was because Thorne's views were more radical than many of his colleagues. For example, he opposed the insurance principle of the National Health Insurance Scheme of 1911 because he felt that low paid workers would not be able to afford the contributions; he also supported George Lansbury when he resigned as a Labour MP and stood as an Independent on the issue of votes for women.

Will Thorne was, and remained, a good constituency MP. But he saw himself primarily as a workers' representative, raising trade union questions and bringing up in Parliament resolutions passed at the TUC Congress. To Thorne, Parliament was an important extension of his trade union activities but it could never be more than that. His Trade Union came first.

Chapter 5

The Years of Fulfilment

For Thorne, as for his union, the years from 1910 to 1920 were ones of achievement and fulfilment.

In 1910, the number of members in the Gasworkers' Union was under 32,000 (less than it had been at the end of 1889). By 1920, the membership of the Gasworkers (whose title had been symbolically changed by the 1916 Biennial Congress to that of the General Workers' Union) had climbed dramatically to well over 450,000. It had become one of the three largest unions in the country and accounted for one in twenty of a total trade union membership, now grown to eight and a half million. The combined membership of the four largest general unions had risen as high as one in eight of all trade unionists. In 1910, Thorne was important, primarily, for the ideas he represented. By 1920, his post of General Secretary of the great General Workers' Union and his position as the best-known leader of a strong bloc of general unions meant that he was a power in the land.

In 1920, the trade union movement was far more influential than it had been in 1910. This was not just because of increased trade union membership. It was also due to the added importance that labour had acquired during the 1914–18 war. An industrial nation at war needs the support of labour to keep its munition factories going. The trade unions, aided by the growing self-confidence and militancy of the shop floor, effectively exploited their new bargaining strength not only to improve the living standards of their members but also to build up a national system of collective bargaining. In this expansion of trade union power and influence, Thorne and the General Workers' Union played an important part.

Politically, the years between 1910 and 1920 were also crucial. In 1910, the Labour Party had been little more than a trade union pressure group, without a really distinctive programme and purpose of its own. By 1920, though still small (only fifty-seven endorsed Labour candidates were returned at the 1918 election), the Labour Party had become the main opposition party both in Parliament and in the country. It was also committed to a Socialist programme. The General Workers made an important contribution to this change. Thorne, himself, had consistently argued for a 'Socialist' party; there were five General Worker MPs in the 1918 Parliament; while Clynes, the President of the Union, had been highly successful as Food Controller in Lloyd George's coalition government and was to be elected Chairman of the Parliamentary Labour Party in 1921 (though he was replaced in 1922 when Ramsay MacDonald returned to Parliament).

For the Gasworkers, the decade began on a sombre note. At the January 1910 Executive meeting, Thorne commented on the heavy permanent charges the union had to bear and said that 'the time had come when means should be devised to either increase the income or reduce the expenditure'.[1] At the Union's Biennial Congress in May of that year, J. E. Smith, the Leeds District Secretary, successfully moved, as Chairman of the Executive, a report that recommended a reduction in both strike benefit and in the disablement benefit that had been introduced in 1904. In the debate on the report, one delegate questioned another item of union expenditure suggesting that a reason for the financial decline was the number of officials the Union had to support and the cost of Parliamentary elections. Later the same delegate criticised Thorne and Clynes for receiving two salaries from the union, the first for their official work, the second for their parliamentary duties. In reply, Thorne explained the considerable expense of being a Member of Parliament, while Clynes pointed out that he and Thorne received less than other Labour Members.[2] In fact, the main reason for the Union's financial difficulties was not so much the number of officials the Union supported (the Union had only fifteen full-time officials) or the cost of political activity (though two general elections in 1910 were expensive) but the decline in union membership during a period of unemployment. In his General Secretary's Report to his union's congress, Thorne gloomily pointed out that, since January 1908, the Union had lost 8,000 members and had dropped to under 32,000.

Yet, in reality, the Union was on the threshold of an unparalleled

1. Will Thorne's original certificate of membership.

2. Will Thorne with Ramsay MacDonald—1923.

3. An Impression of the Battle of Wortley Bridge during the Big Leeds Gas
Strike.

4. Poster Specially Designed by Walter Crane for the Gasworkers and General Labourers' Union for their Annual Demonstration on Children's Sunday.

5. Banner. The National Union of General Workers, whose banner is shown here, was one of the three unions which amalgamated in 1924 to form the National Union of General and Municipal Workers. The other two were the National Amalgamated Union of Labour and the Municipal Employees' Association.

6. Will Thorne, M.P.

expansion. After 1910, membership increased substantially every year, so that, by the end of the June quarter of 1914, the number of members had quadrupled to over 132,000. What were the reasons for this membership expansion—an expansion which was faster (with the exception of the Workers' Union) than that of any other union during this period of trade union growth?

Historians used to believe that the National Insurance Act of 1911 acted as a spur to the increase in union membership. Under this Act, workers were obliged to join 'approved societies' for health insurance purposes. Though Thorne was against the insurance principle, the Gasworkers' Union took advantage of the concession wrested from Lloyd George by the trade unions (who had wanted to establish their own approved societies both as a defensive measure against the non-trade-union societies and also to promote a new incentive for joining trade unions) and set up its own approved society. But the Gasworkers, whose membership had increased by over 40,000 in 1911, went up by only 6,000 in 1912, the year in which they had enrolled 45,000 members in their new approved society.[3] From this evidence, it does not seem likely that the Act had any great effect on trade union membership.

A much more important factor was the economic recovery. By 1911, it was obvious to Gasworker officials that the situation was improving. All districts reported both a rise in membership and more wage increases successfully negotiated on behalf of their workers. In fact, the British economy was now growing fast—and the boom continued until the outbreak of the war.

Though the reduction in unemployment provided a beneficial background to the expansion of trade union membership, it does not explain why it rose so explosively. For that, we must turn to the new militancy of the workers and the aggressive tactics of the trade unions. Commenting on the new labour unrest in his report to the 1912 Biennial Congress of his Union, Thorne suggested that 'the real cause of industrial ferment is the rapid increase in wealth production on the one side and the extra cost of living on the other, which reduces the purchasing power of the wages of the workers'.[4] After 1909, the pace of inflation quickened. Between 1909 and 1913 the cost of living rose by nine per cent;[5] it was only union militancy which prevented an erosion of living standards. Thorne stressed trade union efforts. He wrote 'To my mind it is clear that the organising work put into the movement has been the means of educating the rank and file of the wage earners to rebel

65

against the domination of the master classes'; and added with cautious optimism: 'I do not think we shall get the same indifference displayed in the near future as was apparent three or four years ago, and after the wage earners' revolt in 1889 and 1890'.[6]

As to the new aggression by trade unions, the Gasworkers' Union was deeply involved in the great wave of strikes and unrest of these years. Thorne wrote with enthusiasm of the new Transport Workers' Federation, formed by Tom Mann and Ben Tillett in March 1911 and which the Gasworkers joined immediately. The union also played its part in the great dock strikes of 1911 and 1912 led by the Federation. In December 1913, the Gasworkers were the major union in a second full-scale strike against the Leeds Corporation. Earlier, in June, the Gasworkers had won advances for their own members by a short strike. In the autumn, they joined with other unions to submit a claim on behalf of all corporation employees. The corporation rejected the claim and 4,000 workers came out on strike. However, the Corporation, backed by the Vice-Chancellor of Leeds University, employed large numbers of strike breakers and, by threatening to sack all the strikers, forced the other unions to capitulate. The Gasworkers remained out on strike, but, by the middle of January 1914, had to settle—largely on management's terms. In 1914, the Union, with its growing membership in the building industry, was also involved in the London building industry lockout which lasted over six months. Though many of these strikes were unsuccessful (and Thorne continually warned the members of the dangers of spontaneous, unplanned strikes), they did not deter workers from joining the Union. On the contrary, union aggressiveness and the wage increases secured by it in many industries actually attracted new membership.

The reason why the general unions, particularly the Gasworkers and the Workers' Union, benefited most was because they were able to bring union organisation into the areas of employment with the largest numbers of unorganised workers—the unskilled and semi-skilled in what had been traditional craft industries (like engineering and shipbuilding) and the new mass-production industries (such as chemical, rubber, brick-making, and cement).[7] It was to Thorne's credit that the organisational framework of branches and districts which he had built up during the difficult years enabled the Union to take advantage of the new situation.

A comparison between the 1910 and 1914 balance sheets of the three largest districts (Lancashire, London, and Northern) shows that, by 1914, there had been a dramatic increase not only in the size of existing branches but also in the number of branches catering for new types of membership. In the Lancashire district, for example, existing gasworker branches had expanded enormously and new ones had been created; there were also branches for chemical and textile workers. In the London district there was a great expansion of existing gasworker branches and also the setting up of new branches in the South of England and in East Anglia, including some for building and engineering workers and many for general workers. In the Northern district (from which a new Scottish region had been created in 1913), the size and number of branches catering for unskilled shipyard workers had increased dramatically. Even in the Midlands, where the Workers' Union had achieved a notable success in the expanding engineering and metal industries, the Gasworkers also benefited. Thus the years from 1911 to 1914 saw a decisive breakthrough for the Gasworkers, from their secure base in the gas industry, into new fields.

Though Thorne believed in controlled union aggression and was gratified, even astonished, by its results in the years from 1911 to 1914, he did not accept the fashionable syndicalist arguments of the period. In his report to the 1912 Gasworkers' Congress, he wrote: 'My old colleague, Tom Mann, is now trying to persuade the wage earners not to have anything to do with Parliamentary action. I have always been in favour of direct action on Trade Union lines, because the immediate grievances of the wage earners can be dealt with, but at the same time I am not prepared to allow the employing classes to keep and have control over the political machinery; the combined forces of Labour, and the political working-class movement, marching forward together, can, in my opinion, do a great deal more for the wage earners of the country than can be done if we only concentrate our energies to direct action.' [8] And a resolution from the London district calling for 'the severance of our Members of Parliament from the Labour Party', was defeated comfortably at the Congress.[9] To Thorne, the answer lay not in the abandonment of working-class politics but in a more powerful and more Socialist Labour Party. In his presidential address to the 1912 TUC, Thorne said, in reply to both his own trade union colleagues on the left and the capitalists on the right: 'We might as well expect the lion to represent the lamb, or the highwayman his victim, as to

67

expect the classes who live upon rent, interest and profit to represent those from whose unpaid labour these are drawn. The composition of the House of Commons must be changed. It can be changed when the wage-earners so desire because they have the power in their hands. The employing classes, even with the best will in the world, will not give the workers their political freedom; that we must fight for ourselves. Therefore, the working class political movement must be independent of all political parties, using such political power as the working class today possess to capture the political machinery to enable them to become masters of the economic resources and all the material means of production.' [10]

In personal terms, 1912 was an important year for Thorne. It was the year of his presidency of the Trade Union Congress, the reward for eighteen years of service on the TUC Parliamentary Committee. The President of Congress not only chaired Congress but also the Parliamentary Committee for the year previous. The Parliamentary Committee of that time had, of course, far less power than today's General Council (created in 1921); it was primarily a body which ensured that Congress resolutions were brought to the attention of the relevant government departments. Thorne was an efficient and diligent chairman. He acted as a powerful chief spokesman on railway nationalisation and unemployment when the Parliamentary Committee was politely received, though without results, by the Liberal Prime Minister, Asquith. He also used his chairmanship to organise mass rallies in a number of towns on the eight-hour day. At the 1912 TUC Congress, Thorne proved an effective president, controlling the proceedings with a firmness and good humour which was respected by delegates (in his autobiography, Thorne noted that delegates called him the 'Little Tsar' for his punctuality in starting and carrying on the proceedings).

However, undoubtedly, the high point of Thorne's presidency was his address to the TUC Congress. His speech, which according to the 1912 Congress report, was 'frequently punctuated by hearty signs of approval from the delegates', not only reported, as was customary, on the activities of the Parliamentary Committee during the past year; it also provided both an eloquent summary of Thorne's social and political beliefs and a rallying call for the increasingly strong body of trade unionists throughout the country. In it, Thorne commented on the miners' and dockers' strikes of that year and on the need to continue the battle for social justice: 'Labour unrest cannot cease, nor can the tide of industrial revolt be stemmed until remedial measures are brought about and the present social inequalities removed'. Apart from calling for social and political, as well as industrial action, he emphasised in particular, the inequalities of wealth and of educational opportunity. And he bravely put his personal prestige behind Home Rule for Ireland, so that 'the Irish people can have the opportunity to develop their own national resources and work out their economic and industrial salvation'.

Thorne concluded with his view of the fundamental objectives of the trade union movement. 'The object of all wage-earners should be the collective ownership of the land, railways, and the means of production and transit. The sooner society takes over these essential things the sooner they will come into the possession of those to whom they justly belong. Individual ownership of the means of livelihood has resulted in the economic enslavement of a large portion of society—the working class. It has given to the classes the power to exploit the labour force of the masses; it has also made them masters of political power by means of which they maintain the system and perpetuate the domination over their fellows. I quite recognise the hugeness of their task. But the workers have the power if they have the will, although it may take many years to bring about these objectives. If the sting of present poverty, with the dread of worse poverty in the near future, and recollections of it in the past cannot rouse the workers to action, pen and tongue will not do it. Freedom will mean struggle and sacrifice, which, though hard for the few to sustain, will be light enough for each when all are ready and willing to share it. The workers know this already, and it now remains to be acted upon.' At the end of his speech, Thorne 'resumed his seat amid an enthusiastic burst of cheering'.[11] He had eloquently and powerfully summed up the beliefs and experiences of nearly fifty years.

1912 was also important to Thorne in another way; it marked the beginning of a partnership that was not only to shape the destiny of the Gasworkers for many years to come but also to make a substantial contribution to the Labour movement as a whole. J. E. Smith, previously chairman of the Union, died just before the 1912 Union Congress, and the Lancashire district secretary, J. R. Clynes, was elected unopposed as the new chairman. Clynes' flair for organisation had made Lancashire one of the most powerful districts (by 1914, it had become the largest), and his ability to speak and write clearly and present complicated arguments in simple terms provided Thorne with an ally whose qualities were complementary to Thorne's own.

Clynes, elected in 1906 as Member of Parliament for Manchester North-East, had already begun to make a reputation as a politician. In 1909, he was chairman of the Labour Party and in 1911 he made a notable speech on unemployment in the House of Commons on a Labour amendment to the King's Speech. His growing national prestige made him useful to the Gasworkers, not only for recruitment rallies up and down the country, but also as a 'trouble-shooter'. During the December 1913 Leeds Corporation strike, it was Clynes who got the Union and its members 'off the hook' by negotiating a settlement which, if not satisfactory, was at least better than the total humiliation that might otherwise have occurred. It is interesting that the Corporation, which had refused to meet the strikers' local leaders, agreed to meet Clynes because of his 'known moderation'.[12] Clynes, a member of the ILP, was by temperament more moderate in his views than Thorne; already he had joined, in an individual capacity, the government's Industrial Council, a body of prominent employers and union officials set up in 1911 to arbitrate in disputes, whereas Thorne had declined to do so, because, as he told the TUC Parliamentary Committee, it might limit the right to strike.[13]

Despite differences of emphasis, Thorne and Clynes together formed one of the most formidable and effective partnerships in the Labour movement. Thorne certainly needed support. The dramatic increase in membership had put a heavy burden on him, already fifty-five years old in 1912. The Gasworkers, however, were slower than the Workers' Union in reacting to the rapid growth of membership. While the latter, more adventurous in approach, were always ready to appoint new officers and open up new districts, the Gasworkers' bitter experience of the hard years after 1890 inclined them to caution. The increase in the number of organisers authorised by the 1912 Union Congress was hardly enough to keep pace with the demands of organising work, of the numerous disputes with which the union was involved, and of the growing number of cases under the Workmen's Compensation Act of 1906, which had extended to all workers compensation for industrial injuries. The Executive also waited until 1913, when the Gasworkers had over 5,000 members in Scotland, before it authorised the creation of a new district there. Clynes took some of the burden off Thorne's shoulders—and the union leadership became a duumvirate. In 1914, Clynes' new role was confirmed by the creation of a new post of paid President (which, however, he did not take up until 1916).

By the outbreak of war, the Gasworkers had become one of the five largest unions in the country, while the prestige of Thorne and its President, Clynes, had reached new heights. The war was to confirm and strengthen the position of the Gasworkers and its leaders.

The First World War was a turning point in Thorne's life. He took the view, one which he was to hold consistently throughout, that, once hostilities had been declared, the trade unions should do all that was in their power to support the Allied cause. Thorne was proud of his internationalism. As he told a Labour Party Conference in 1917, he had attended as many Socialist Internationals as any member of the Labour Party.[14] However, already some years before the war, he had shared Hyndman's scepticism about German intentions, in general, and about the ability of the German Social Democrats, in particular, to prevent German aggression; and his introduction of the Citizen Army Bill in Parliament reflected a realism about the prospects for international peace. Certainly, he hoped fervently that peace would continue, and, if the war had been only between a militaristic Germany and a despotic Russia, Thorne, like many others on the left, would have wished Britain to have stayed out. But, as Clynes stated, the key issue for the majority in both the Labour Party and the trade union movement was French involvement and, above all, the successful German attack on neutral Belgium: 'Had the Germans been flung back from the French and Belgian frontiers in the early weeks of the war, it is possible that British Labour might have hesitated further over its attitude towards the coming struggle. But, with the future of our country actually in danger, the time for deliberation was past. Blame could be apportioned later; the immediate task before us all was to save England from invasion.'[15]

On 24 August 1914, the Joint Board—the Liaison Committee of the Labour Party, the General Federation of Trade Unions, and the Parliamentary Committee of which Thorne was a member, agreed that an immediate effort be made to terminate all existing disputes and that a serious attempt should be made to solve any disputes that arose during the war period. Five days later, the Labour

71

Party agreed to an electoral truce, and, on 2 September, the Parliamentary Committee followed the lead of the Labour Party in backing national recruiting efforts for the armed forces. Thus, within a month of the declaration of war, the Labour movement had given its support to the government.

Thorne threw himself whole-heartedly behind the war effort. Throughout the war period, he consistently argued that nothing should detract from its winning. In his report for the March quarter of 1915, he wrote: 'Be the fight long or short, I feel quite sure that those in the fighting line, those who are being made fit to take a place at the front, and those in civil life at home will not think about peace proposals until every German soldier has been withdrawn from Belgium and France, either voluntarily or by force.' He added: 'It is certain that not one member of the union would do anything to prevent our gallant soldiers from being fully supplied with all necessary equipment'.[16] Thorne and Clynes spoke at a number of recruiting meetings; and, when it became clear during 1915 that conscription would be required, Thorne told his members that 'seeing that the people of this country, including trade unionists, have sent their sons, brothers and other relatives to fight in a just cause (Thorne's own son was at the front and later killed at Ypres) I cannot believe that the general opinion is against applying compulsion to those who can serve, and who have hung back up till the present time'.[17] At the 1916 Biennial Congress, Thorne, in answer to criticism from the floor, replied that he belonged to the school which thought it was the duty of wage-earners to prosecute the war to a successful termination, and that it was quite impossible to obtain a sufficient number of men by the ordinary voluntary methods. He pointed out that 'the voluntary method was not fair to the working class' and that 'if some form of compulsion had not been introduced a great number of the middle class would still have been out of the Army'.[18] As a symbol of his commitment, Thorne even joined the West Ham Volunteer Force and was given the rank of Lieutenant-Colonel—a rank which, as his autobiography implies, gave him some innocent pride but which was anathema to his anti-war critics in the borough.

Thorne's views on the war separated him from some of his former allies on the left and, in particular, involved him in a running fight with the ILP. The leaders of the ILP, including Ramsay MacDonald, who had to resign his leadership of the Parliamentary Labour Party, considered that Britain should have remained out of the war and the Labour Movement aloof from the war effort because it was the wrong war fought for the wrong reason. Clynes, despite the fact that he remained a member of the ILP, escaped lightly (in 1918 he was returned unopposed at Manchester North-East); but the ILP leaders, particularly Snowden, did not forgive Thorne for his outspokenness.

Thorne was personally attacked in the ILP newspaper, the *Labour Leader*, by Snowden in the most bitter terms. He wrote sneeringly of Thorne's 'unlettered ignorance and unfitness for Parliament'. This attack was deeply resented not only by Thorne (he wrote later that the episode was 'the only one in my career which really threatened to affect my spirit' [19]) but also by his own Union colleagues. Thorne relates how, at a social gathering during the Union's 1916 Biennial Congress, the audience rose and cheered him, while the General Council of the Union condemned the article in a letter to the *Labour Leader*: 'Instead of taunting Labour spokesmen with the lack of an educated manner', the General Council complained, 'you ought to sympathise with and sustain men who as boys had to work at hard labour when for years they should have been at school. Anyhow, against the polish of whoever writes your paragraphs, we set the splendid pioneer work of Mr Thorne as an educationalist agitator to secure for every working lad the schooling advantages of which he was deprived.' [20] The *Labour Leader* also unfairly attacked the General Workers for neglecting their obligations to a Lancashire District Organiser, Charles Dukes, who, though a conscientious objector, had been first compelled to serve in the army and then court-martialled for breaches of army discipline. As Clynes pointed out to the Union's General Council, Dukes had, in fact, written a letter to Thorne and Clynes expressly thanking them for their efforts to secure exemption for him. [21]

Given Thorne's views, it was natural that he should support Hyndman in his pro-war policy when, in 1916, he broke with the majority of the British Socialist Party (which the SDF had become in 1911).

Thorne's opinion on the war did not, however, mean that he had forgotten his commitment to the working class. On the contrary, he saw, from the first, that the war created a new situation in which the Labour Movement was bound to become more powerful and would, therefore, be in a stronger position to improve the conditions of the workers. From the start of the war, Thorne's language became more aggressive. In December 1914, he complained that 'when the war began the Government could not come quickly enough to the rescue of the bankers, railway directors, and the dividend receiving classes, but where the working-class interests are concerned great reluctance is shown to deal with those who are getting huge fortunes by fleecing the poorest people'. He added 'it seems to me that there are a number of "Kaisers" in this country who should be brought to book for the betterment of the world'.[22] In March 1915, he fulminated against 'the food and fuel Kaisers' and bitterly criticised the fact that 'the newspaper owners who have chastised workmen about drink and neglect of work would never think of lecturing the shipowners, colliery proprietors, wheat merchants, and the meat bosses who are extracting millions of money out of the pockets of the poor by jumping prices of food and fuel'.[23] During 1915 and 1916, he asked a number of pointed questions in the House of Commons about prices and about the profit which some contractors were making out of the armed forces. In an eloquent passage in his quarterly report for September 1915, Thorne asked whether any section of the community was doing more for the nation than the class to which he and his members belonged. 'What are the women and children of the upper classes doing? Are they being mentally and physically exhausted by excessive labour? Are they turning out of their comfortable homes to work on these cold and cheerless mornings? Are their children labouring in the factory, mill and field? When rich people talk about the sacrifices they are making, let us remind them of what the workers and their wives and children are silently doing for the country in this terrible struggle.'[24]

It was the government's desperate need of munitions for the army, bogged down in a prolonged and bloody trench war, which gave the trade union movement and, in particular, the general unions a new opportunity. Once it became obvious that the war would not be over quickly, both Asquith and Lloyd George realised the critical importance of labour to the war effort. In May 1915, Asquith invited the Labour Party to join a Coalition government. After some hesitation, the Labour leader, Henderson, accepted a place in the Cabinet, while two other Labour MPs received less important government posts. Clynes took the minority view that Asquith was not offering the Labour Party enough to make a coalition worthwhile. Earlier in March, Lloyd George, then Chancellor of the Exchequer, had made the so-called 'Treasury' agreement with trade union leaders (including Thorne) by which, in return for compulsory arbitration and the 'dilution' of skilled labour by substituting less skilled workers and women, the government agreed to control profits of munition firms. When Lloyd George became Minister of Munitions in June 1915, he immediately introduced legislation (which became the Munitions Act in the following month) giving backing to the 'Treasury Agreement'.

While Thorne was prepared to accept arbitration and welcomed the government's control of profits, he believed that 'the government, after recognising the failure of the capitalist, should have taken the production of munitions entirely out of private hands, and worked the establishments with the cooperation of trade union representatives for the benefit of the state; and he warned that 'after what has been sacrificed, if the Government attempt in the near future to impose further burdens upon the poorer classes by taxing food or wages, we shall resist by every means at our command'.[25]

In practice, the Munitions Act did not stop strikes but it did enable the general unions to spread their organisation to unskilled workers. 'Dilution' of labour brought these workers into engineering. In addition, under the system of compulsory arbitration, trade unions could force employers to negotiate with them, and officials at the Ministry of Munitions also put pressure on employers to give trade union officials recruiting facilities.

At first, 'dilution' was largely confined to the introduction of women into factories making shells and fuses, as had been agreed between the Amalgamated Society of Engineers and the engineering employers in March 1915. But Thorne, who had told the Webbs before the war that women were impossible to organise,[26] realised that 'dilution' gave the Union the opportunity, as never before, to recruit women workers. In his quarterly report of March 1916, he told his members that the Union would not be able to increase its membership during the war 'unless we enrol the large number of women who are entering the industrial field to take the place of men'.[27] As recruitment for the front stepped up, so the Union had to run very hard not to stand still. At the end of 1915, membership was no higher than two years before. In 1916 and 1917, however, the government applied dilution in the munitions industries more seriously. By 1918, there were 600,000 women employed in these industries. The union membership responded; by December 1916, the total had risen to 152,000 and, by the end of 1917, to 256,000.

The importance of female membership was reflected in the increasing interest displayed in their conditions by the Union. As the Scottish District Secretary wrote in 1916, 'It is our duty to make room for them amongst us, to protect them from becoming instrumental in breaking down the standard of rates and conditions ... the future of our union will depend very largely upon our appreciation of this very important factor.' [28] Together with the National Federation of Women Workers, led by Mary Macarthur and Margaret Bondfield, and the Workers' Union, amongst others, the Union forced the government in January 1916 to amend the Munitions Act, so that employers had to apply the appropriate men's rates to women employed on men's work. A special tribunal was also set up to decide women's rates on women's work. To exploit its success, the union issued a leaflet, appealing to women workers; and districts were supplied with copies of the Ministry of Munition's regulations governing rates of pay of women in controlled factories and of the Ministry's letter giving encouragement to women to join trade unions. Throughout the war, Thorne and Clynes continued to press the Minister of Munitions on women's wages. Although the Union can be criticised for its caution in failing to appoint a National Woman Organiser, districts were empowered to use women speakers or organisers 'where such service could be utilised to advantage in any special efforts being made'.[29]

Thorne's Union also became a champion of the power-paid munitions workers. The January 1916 amendment to the Munitions Act gave legal force to the already accepted practice that members of the general unions employed on jobs previously carried out by skilled men were paid the local skilled rate. But other workers depended on labourers' rates, though with additions for semi-skilled work. The local bargaining machinery proved hopelessly inadequate to cope with the demands of lower-paid workers, whose wage increases had been eroded by dramatic price increases of 1915 and 1916.[30]

Throughout 1916, the Union reports reflected the demand for some action to be taken by the government. Clynes wrote that 'the appeals made by low-paid workmen for redress against the burden of the high cost of living deserve better treatment from the government and from employers'.[31] The Union, after Thorne had written to the Minister of Munitions on 24 July 1916 asking for a general advance for low-paid workers, decided that the best course of action was to present a joint claim with the Workers'

Union and the other general unions at national level. After some delay, the general unions' initiative was successful and, in March 1917, the first ever national flat rate increase (which gave the lower paid the highest relative advance) was implemented, with a further review to be made every four months.

Thorne and Clynes won another victory for the less skilled in 1917 when they were largely instrumental in forcing the government to reverse the 'trade-card' system. Under this system (which the government had introduced in response to a strike of skilled workers in the autumn of 1916), the skilled unions alone could issue their members with 'trade cards' which exempted them from military service. Though once conscription was introduced there had to be some system of exemptions for 'key' munition workers, the 'trade card' system was blatantly unfair to the less skilled workers, who, in many cases, were, through 'dilution', now doing skilled work, and to the general unions, who had to watch while the skilled unions exempted all their own members, including the less-skilled, whom they were now beginning to recruit. On 14 December 1916, the Union's Executive empowered Thorne and Clynes to make representations to the government on behalf of their own members. Throughout the early months of 1917, the two leaders mounted a high pressure campaign, using every channel open to them, including questions in the House of Commons, letters to the Ministry of Munitions, deputations, with other unions, to the War Office, the Ministry of Munitions, and the Directorate of National Service, and, perhaps most important of all, a direct appeal to their Labour colleague, Arthur Henderson, now an influential member of the War Cabinet. The Union insisted that it was not seeking any special privilege for its members but was asking merely that 'men shall be treated alike irrespective of trade unions'.[32] Their campaign was successful. In May 1917, the trade card system was abandoned and replaced by a schedule of reserved occupations, by which men were exempted according to their job and not through their union card.

The new power of the general unions and, in particular, of the Gasworkers' Union (who had changed their name at the 1916 Biennial Congress to the General Workers' Union, to bring it into line with current realities) was reflected in a number of ways.

In July 1917, the General Labourers' National Council, which had been set up in 1907, was transformed into a more effective body, the National Federation of General Workers, with Clynes as its President, to co-ordinate at national level the bargaining of its members. In the engineering industry, the Engineers and eight smaller craft unions agreed to recognise the right of the General Workers' Union to organise the semi-skilled workers and labourers. Though some of the driving force behind this was the Engineers' suspicion that the Workers' Union, led by Duncan and Beard, were accepting skilled men into membership at a contribution less than half that of the Engineers, it was also a recognition of the new importance of the General Workers' Union in the engineering industry.

Perhaps most striking of all was Clynes' appointment in May 1917 as Parliamentary Secretary to the Food Ministry. Both Clynes (who had opposed the first coalition) and Thorne voted for Labour's acceptance of office in Lloyd George's new Coalition government, formed in December 1916. Lloyd George had offered the Labour Party much better terms than had Asquith, including state control of mines and shipping, the introduction of food rationing, and, amongst other ministerial appointments, a seat for Arthur Henderson in a small War Cabinet. Clynes and Thorne both took the view that, though they disapproved of the methods used to pull down the Asquith government, the situation was so grave that a more vigorous lead was needed, and that the Labour Movement ought to give its full backing to the new government. When, in the following year, Lloyd George, at the suggestion of Lord Rhondda, the new Food Controller, invited Clynes to become Parliamentary Secretary, the union Executive gave him full backing, 'believing that in accepting the position Brother Clynes rightly took an opportunity of serving working-class interests'.[33] Clynes proved himself in his successful introduction of rationing and was also responsible for the setting up of a Consumers' Council—a novel concept—to keep the Ministry of Food in touch with public opinion, so that, when Lord Rhondda died in July 1918, Clynes was his natural successor as Food Controller. It was right that the President of the General Workers' Union, whose members were amongst the lower paid and who were therefore hardest hit by price increases, should have played a major part in taming the speculators and controlling food prices.

1917—the year of the two Russian revolutions and entry of the United States into the war—was a critical year both for the course of the war and for the future of the British Labour Movement. The Russian Revolution of March 1917, which overthrew the Tsar, was naturally welcomed throughout the Labour Movement. Later that month, Thorne was asked by Lloyd George, together with another trade unionist, James O'Grady (who became Secretary of the National Federation of General Workers later in 1917) to form an official deputation 'to convey a congratulatory message and fraternal greetings to the new Russian government'.[34] Thorne could have been excused if he had refused. Obviously there was some personal danger involved in the sea voyage. He could not have forgotten that the vessel in which the war leader Kitchener had been travelling to Russia in 1916 had been sunk, and Kitchener and most of the crew drowned. By spring 1917, one ship in every four leaving British ports failed to return.[35] But Thorne, who had always been passionately interested in the development of democracy in Russia, promptly accepted. The deputation was then backed by the Labour Party, the TUC, and his own union.

The night Thorne left, he met, by chance, the Conservative politician, F. E. Smith (later Lord Birkenhead). Smith insisted that, because of the cold in Russia, Thorne should borrow his own luxurious fur coat. Thorne accepted with thanks. Immediately afterwards he was seen by one of his colleagues wearing the coat and instantly became a subject of 'tea room' gossip in the House of Commons. This incident was later that year used against him by anti-war critics in his constituency—a reminder that the most harmless gestures can be misinterpreted by political enemies.

Thorne and his party reached Russia safely, though he was surprised to be shadowed until Stockholm by 'two of the expensive and unnecessary Secret Service agents maintained by our Government'.[36] His journey through a shattered and chaotic Russia made a deep impression on him. He visited Petrograd (later renamed Leningrad), Moscow, Minsk, spoke at many meetings, and met a number of politicians, including Kerensky, who he found charming but weak. Describing his experiences some years later, he remembered his surprise at finding that the majority of representatives on the Petrograd Soviet were intellectuals; and recalled a two-hour speech Lenin (who had just arrived from Geneva) made to the Soviet. In the report which he and his colleagues prepared for the War Cabinet, Thorne underlined the uncertainties of the Russian internal situation and warned that there was a growing body of opinion in the Soviet against the war, which he attributed

79

to the German propaganda and 'the Jewish element' (presumably the Bolsheviks). He stressed the need for Britain to be closely involved in Russian affairs, if Russia were to remain in the war.[37]

On his return to Britain, Thorne reported to Lloyd George and saw King George V at Buckingham Palace (in 1913, he had refused to appear at the official opening by the King of a new reservoir in his constituency, because the King's visit to the East End would not assist in removing 'the deep-rooted and chronic poverty in the Borough').[38] When the King, alarmed by the revolution in Russia and the recent conference at Leeds of the United Socialist Council which had called for the setting up of British Soviets, asked whether there would be a similar upheaval in Britain, Thorne calmed him by replying that there would not be 'a physical violent revolution'. He warned the King, however, that there would have to be 'many political and industrial changes within the course of the next few years'.[39]

The example of the first Russian revolution was certainly one factor in the considerable growth in British industrial unrest during 1917. In May, following the government's withdrawal of the 'trade-card system' and a decision to extend 'dilution' to work outside the state munitions factories, shop stewards from the craft unions led a number of protest strikes that threatened the war effort. Though the leaders of the movement claimed to speak for all munitions workers, only in the Sheffield area did members of the general unions take part. The Executive of the General Workers, however, gave financial support to all members who had been stopped from working because of the strikes. The government, thoroughly alarmed, set up Commissions of Inquiry into the industrial unrest in different parts of the country, which showed that many trade unionists, particularly in the craft unions, had lost confidence in the government and in their own leaders. Lloyd George gave in to the craft unions over 'dilution' and also abolished the leaving Certificate system, set up by the Munitions Act, by which it was illegal for munitions workers to leave their jobs without the employer's permission.

As part of the package and in order to prevent skilled time workers leaving to seek higher paid jobs elsewhere, the government also announced, in October 1917, a $12\frac{1}{2}$ per cent addition on rates of skilled time workers. This last concession to the skilled workers aroused the fury of the semi-skilled and unskilled, many of whom were also on time rates. Thorne, after meeting the Minister of Munitions, together with leaders of the Workers' Union, used the machinery of the National Federation of General Workers. The NFGW decided to threaten to ballot their members on a national strike if the increase was not extended to their members. The government gave way (an agreement was signed directly between the NFGW and the War Cabinet [40]) and awarded the semi-skilled and skilled workers a 12½ per cent wage increase similar to that of the skilled workers. Because of successful pressure, the low-paid piece workers were also given an increase of 7½ per cent. Conscious of their new power, the General Workers and the other general unions used the 12½ per cent award to bargain for national increases in other industries.

Another feature of the 1917 unrest was the activity of the shop stewards of the General Workers' Union. At the 1916 Biennial Congress, a delegate from Leeds, moving a resolution calling for an increase in the commission paid to collecting stewards from 7½ to 10 per cent, stated that shop stewards 'were mainly instrumental in keeping the members together'.[41] Though by rule, the shop stewards' job was merely to collect contributions, in practice, particularly since the beginning of the war, they had usually done much more. In response to demands from the Sheffield district in May 1917, the Union's General Council laid down a 'code of by-laws', defining their duties and also the rules for the setting up of shop committees in the Sheffield district and other industrial centres. The union also signed an agreement with the engineering employers that recognised the role of the shop steward in the disputes machinery of the industry. Clynes and Thorne disagreed on the shop steward issue. At a General Council meeting in November 1917, which discussed the relationship of the shop stewards to the Union, Clynes, who was a member of the Whitley Committee on Joint Industrial Councils (set up by the coalition government in 1916 to consider industrial relations after the war) argued that the Works Committees proposed by the Whitley Committee were preferable as they would work 'under proper instructions from the trade unions' and would eventually take the place of shop stewards.[42] Thorne, though concerned lest precipitate and ill co-ordinated action by inexperienced shop stewards should waste union resources and cause hardship to the members, was convinced they were a valuable asset to the Union.[43]

However, the most important long-term effect of the Russian revolutions was on the development of the Labour Party. It was to Henderson's credit that he saw the opening that the new climate created for the labour movement. Henderson, who, following

Thorne's mission, was sent to Russia in May by the War Cabinet to advise on the best means of keeping Russia in the war, came back convinced that, in view of the deteriorating situation there, the right course for the British government was to seek a negotiated peace. Accordingly, he favoured the attendance of the British Labour Party at a Socialist and Labour Conference to be held at Stockholm and at which representatives of the German and Austrian labour movements would be present, and persuaded a special Labour Party Conference on 10 August 1917 that the party ought to adopt his policy. Whereupon Lloyd George, at the request of the Conservative members of the War Cabinet, reprimanded Henderson (who had previously seemed to agree with him). The leader of the Parliamentary Labour Party immediately resigned from the government.

Though the Labour Party remained in the coalition, the resignation of Henderson was the prelude to the emergence of Labour as a fully independent, national party, committed to a Socialist programme. Over the next year, Henderson, as its Secretary, reunited the party and the Labour Movement as a whole around a new statement of war aims ('Memorandum of War Aims') which looked towards the future and called for a world safe for democracy and an end to war as an instrument of policy. The most notable feature of this influential statement was its demand for the establishment of a League of Nations.

In February 1918, the Labour Party also adopted, for the first time, a Socialist constitution, including the famous Clause Four which called for the common ownership of the means of production. It followed this up in June by endorsing a fuller statement of party policy, *Labour and the New Social Order*, drafted by Sidney Webb, which argued for a national minimum standard for all, democratic control of industry (including nationalisation of railways, mines, electric power, and land), redistribution of wealth and the provision of social services, and an expansion of educational and cultural opportunities—a programme which attractively combined idealism with practical reform. In the words of the American ambassador, 'the Labour Party is already playing for supremacy'.[44]

The attitude of Thorne to the Stockholm Conference was a credit to his consistency, if not to his tactical judgement. While nobody in the Labour Movement was more aware of the need for an independent and Socialist Labour Party, Thorne remained resolutely convinced that nothing useful could come from the

82

proposed Conference. At the August 1917 Labour Party Conference, his Union, at their General Secretary's insistence, voted against sending delegates to Stockholm. As he told the House of Commons later that month, 'I am certain that if this Conference is held at Stockholm you will not get anything out of the German delegates declaring themselves against the Kaiser, or that they are going to democratise Germany'.[45] Though, in fact, the failure of the allied labour movements to agree on war aims, combined with the refusal of their governments to grant passports (which Thorne condemned) prevented the Stockholm Conference taking place, there was much justice in Thorne's assessment of German Social Democratic views—or at least of the majority. When the inter-allied Labour and Socialist Conference in London in February 1918 asked the German Social Democrats for their response to the inter-allied war aims (based on the British Labour Party's memorandum), it received a dusty answer. However, despite Thorne's views, the Union gave full backing to Labour's new war aims, both as a practical programme for world peace and as a basis for party unity. Another illustration of Thorne's belief in the need for unity is that he seconded a compromise resolution on war aims at the TUC conference in September 1917 and also persuaded his union to nominate Henderson and Ramsay MacDonald that year for the posts of Secretary and Treasurer of the Labour Party, respectively. As to the new Socialist programme, the General Workers naturally gave it full backing. It expressed in clear terms the political and social objectives for which their General Secretary had fought all his life.

The December 1918 General Election, which followed the Allied victory, was a minor triumph for the General Workers' Union—if not for the Labour Party. Four financially supported members of the Union—Thorne, Clynes, Jones, and Hayday—and three other non-sponsored members were successful. Before the election, Clynes and Thorne argued that the Labour Party ought to remain in the coalition, so that it could influence the terms of the peace settlement (a view, which, given Lloyd George's need for Labour support at that time, had some logic to it), but the overwhelming majority at a special Labour Party Conference on 14 November voted in favour of withdrawal and Clynes loyally left the coalition. Thorne had had some difficulty in getting re-elected. His anti-war critics, both from the ILP and the British Socialist Party, gained control of his local party and rejected him, despite his long record of service, for his South West Ham constituency. Fortunately for Thorne, he was adopted, with Union support, for the neighbouring constituency of Plaistow, and was elected in 1918 by a comfortable majority, one of only four successful candidates in London. In the country as a whole, Labour received nearly a quarter of the total vote of a greatly expanded electorate, but because of the electoral system, only fifty-seven endorsed Labour members were returned, compared to three hundred and thirty-nine Conservatives, who now dominated the Lloyd George coalition.

The immediate post-war situation was explosive; a government, dominated by Conservatives, who wished to reverse the gains made by labour during the war, and a trade union movement, with the confidence born of success and of its eight and a half million members, determined to resist.

It has been said that the general unions, especially the General Workers, spent the two years after 1918 standing aside from the main current of events in the labour movement.[46] As far as the General Workers' Union was concerned, a perhaps more accurate assessment is that the views of its leaders, Thorne and Clynes, were not always in tune with those of the majority of the movement during this period. There were three major issues between 1918 and 1920 in which the Labour Movement came in conflict with the government—public ownership of the mines and the wages of the miners, the wages of the railway workers, and the government's policy towards Soviet Russia. Government control over the mines and railways during the war meant that, inevitably, any dispute in these industries would bring the unions concerned in direct conflict with the government. The pre-war Triple Industrial Alliance of the Miners' Federation, the National Union of Railwaymen, and the National Transport Workers' Federation (of which the General Workers' Union remained a member) was renewed in February 1919. The Government, faced by demands from the apparently united unions, prevaricated, setting up a Commission of Inquiry into the coal industry and re-opening negotiations with the railwaymen which they had broken off. The short-lived success of the Federation encouraged the trade union leaders, like the Miners' President, Smillie and the Secretary of the Transport Workers' Federation, Williams, in a demand for 'direct action' to force the government to yield to political demands such as the nationalisation of the mines, and non-intervention in Russian affairs. The Council of the Triple Alliance called on the TUC Parliamentary Committee to call a special conference that would, amongst other matters, decide what action should be taken to secure the withdrawal of British troops from Russia.

Thorne and Clynes believed that direct action on political matters was dangerous. In June 1919, at the Annual Council meeting of the Transport Workers' Federation, Thorne spoke against such a political initiative, while at the Labour Conference of that year Clynes reminded delegates of the implications of direct action: 'Were they going to concede to every other class the right they were claiming to exercise? . . . the blow which they were threatening would not be a blow at a Government, but a blow at democracy'.[47] In March 1920, the General Workers voted with the majority at a special TUC Conference against a general strike in support of the workers' demand for coal nationalisation.

The only time the Union supported the threat of direct action on a political matter was in the summer of 1920 over the question of whether or not Britain should intervene on the side of Poland in the Russo-Polish war. It was Clynes who moved the resolution at a special conference approving the formation of a Council of Action (initiated by a new trade union figure, Ernest Bevin) and threatening a general strike if the government used British troops against Soviet Russia. The General Workers were prepared to modify their policy because the issue, which involved not only the right of self-determination of any working-class regime but also that of peace itself, was so overriding. The government, faced not only with a united labour movement but also with a war-weary public opinion, climbed down—though, in any case, the Poles were able to drive the Russians out of Poland without any British help.

The logic of the General Workers' position was that political change was more effectively achieved through the ballot box. In fact, Thorne's views were entirely consistent with the stand he had taken against the syndicalists in 1912; and with the greater strength of the Labour Party after the war (they gained seats at by-elections), the position he supported was becoming increasingly credible. Clynes put the Union viewpoint forcibly at the 1920 Union Congress (Thorne was absent because of a serious illness); 'The new doctrine (of direct action) is preached with a child-like belief in its success as a method for economic reconstruction. We cannot show the failure of political efforts which have never been fully tried at all. Working-class electoral power has only recently become overwhelming, and the means to use that power has only been offered to the workers within the past few years in the form of a well-established national party.'[48] In the opinion of Thorne and Clynes, direct action would only set back the chances of a Labour government—and, in most circumstances, was an inappropriate weapon.

The judgement of Ernest Bevin's biographer on the use of direct action during this period is perhaps the best vindication of the position adopted by Thorne and Clynes: 'The paradox of "direct action" was that the conditions which alone made success possible—the unanimity of the Labour Movement and widespread support outside it—made it also unnecessary, since no government was likely to fly in the face of the opinion of the majority.'[49]

In industrial terms, the two years after the war were highly successful for the General Workers. Building on the success of the National Federation of General Workers during the war and on the impetus created by the Whitley Report, the General Workers took a leading role in evolving a new system of national negotiations in a number of industries, including gas, local authorities, docks, chemicals, rubber, cocoa and chocolate, and flour milling, which was to be vitally important in the future. During the war, Thorne had agreed that, though there were deep conflicts of interest between employers and workers, it could be of advantage to have effective negotiating and conciliating machinery.[50] In 1920, in his Congress Report, he was able to tell union members that he thought money and time spent in the new JICs were worthwhile 'for they provide a method of settling grievances through the medium of the round table conference'.[51] Certainly, the results of collective bargaining, both in terms of improvements in wages and conditions and of a rapidly expanding membership, were most encouraging.

Thorne could have been forgiven for feeling that, as he implied in his reports during 1920, future prospects for the Union were excellent. In fact, the next decade, with its catastrophic unemployment, was to bring crisis to both wings of the labour movement. The Labour Party, despite two minority governments, had no real answer. As for the trades unions, apparently so strong in 1920, expansion became a thing of the past—and many turned to amalgamation to provide themselves with the security that individual unions now lacked.

Chapter 6

The Great Amalgamation

Amalgamation is, in a sense, the natural extension of general unionism. If it is not possible to recruit all workers directly within a single union, then the logical step is to unite with other unions.

In 1889, Thorne had argued for the principle of 'one man, one ticket' in order, as he wrote later, 'to secure the consolidation of the trade union and Labour forces; we wanted to eradicate quarrels between the workers because they belonged to different organisations, and realise the unity and oneness of the working class.'[1] He had also, though without success, suggested to the Union of Coal Porters and the Miners' Federation that they should federate. He explained to his own members that 'with such an organisation, if a strike took place at any gasworks, the coal miners at the pits would be able to prevent coal being sent to the gasworks in dispute, and even if the miners could not do this effectively the coal porters could.'[2]

In his report for 1895, Thorne pointed out that the growing counter-offensive of the employers made it even more essential for the workers themselves to unite. 'Should not this prove to all sections of workers the absolute necessity of joining together?', asked Thorne: 'The time has passed for distinctions being made between the Engineers and the Labourer. ... Is there, then, no possibility of a General Federation being brought about so that all workers may unite in checking the onslaught that is now being made upon them by the Capitalist?'[3] When, in 1897, the TUC decided to form a federation 'to render mutual assistance in disputes, strikes and lockouts', it is significant that the committee set up to investigate the scheme included Pete Curran, the National Organiser of the Gasworkers. The Gasworkers' Union was the second largest to join the General Federation of Trade Unions, set up, as a result of the committee's report, by a special

87

TUC Congress in 1899, and Curran became Chairman. However, the majority of unions did not join and the General Federation did not contribute to the unity for which the Gasworkers aimed. From Thorne's point of view, probably its most important measure was the formation in 1907 of a General Labourers' National Council.

There were, in fact, always serious obstacles to closer unity, as Thorne quickly recognised. As early as 1896, he was complaining that plans for an amalgamation of building labourers' unions created problems. The General Secretary of the United Builders Labourers' Union had argued for an amalgamation, confined only to building labourers. Thorne, in reply, put the classic case for general unionism: 'Does he not perceive that the spirit of the times is for less unions and more unity? Does he not recognise that the Builders Labourers cannot stand alone against the Organised-Capitalism of today? Is he not aware that the chief cause of the success of the Gasworkers and General Labourers Union lies in the fact of there being so many sections of labour attached and not having all the eggs in one basket? . . . Class distinction must be put down and in its place must arise a union of all creeds and nationalities.'[4] However, when in the aftermath of the Engineering Employers' lockout, Tom Mann set up the Workers' Union to organise 'all sections of the community on an industrial and political basis', Thorne pointed out that his own organisation performed both the industrial and political functions proposed for the new union.[5] Understandably, he saw Mann's creation as more a rival than an aid to the unity for which both unions were working.

These two early examples illustrate some of the realities that confront unions which wish to unite. Amalgamation is far easier to discuss than to achieve. In any amalgamation, there are always conflicts—in the level of contributions and benefits, in structure and organisation, in membership interest and location, and, above all, in the philosophy and ambitions of the leaders—which have to be reconciled. Until 1917, there was also the legal position, which required the consent of two-thirds of the membership. In judging the Union's relative lack of success before 1924 and the measure of Thorne's and Clynes' achievement in 1924, the difficulties in the way of amalgamation must always be remembered.

One of the basic ideas that excited trade unionists during the great 'labour unrest' of 1910–14 was that of amalgamation. On his return from Australia (where he had been since 1901), Tom Mann established 'Amalgamation Committees', to agitate for industrial unionism within each industry, and, with Tillet and Havelock Wilson, set up the Transport Workers' Federation. However, amalgamation to promote industrial unionism was not only a challenge to the powerful craft unions but also to the general unions as well.

The Gasworkers immediately joined the Transport Workers Federation. Thorne told his members: 'One of the objects of the Federation is to ensure recognition of cards among members of the societies affiliated. This is a principle the officials of our union have advocated ever since the establishment of the union, and if it had been adopted generally twenty years ago general labourers and kindred unions would be much stronger than they are today.'[6] However, Thorne believed that the type of amalgamation which best suited the principles of general unionism was one with other labourers' unions. At the Gasworkers' 1912 Biennial Congress, he told the members that he was strongly opposed to 'detaching any section of our membership . . . there was a danger that other trades would come along with amalgamation schemes, and eventually we might have to disband altogether'.[7] The Gasworkers, therefore, took the initiative at the General Labourers' National Council (GLNC) and proposed the amalgamation of all general unions; this was overwhelmingly endorsed in principle by a ballot of the membership. In March 1913, Clynes, in one of his periodic articles to Union members, wrote: 'When we have industrial conditions which place different grades of men in superior and subordinate relationship to each other . . . it is futile to talk of forcing all these men into one organisation as though the fact of tradesman and labourer did not exist at all. . . . Labourers' unions cannot, with advantage, be merged at present in the other unions; they can amalgamate their own forces and seek friendly alliance with every other force.'[8]

The Gasworkers put forward detailed proposals for amalgamation at a special committee of the GLNC, chaired by Clynes, but the other general unions were slow in responding. In 1913, the position was further complicated by an approach for amalgamation by the Transport Workers' Federation to the GLNC, some of whose constituents were, like the Gasworkers, members of both bodies. In July 1914, a joint meeting of the two organisations, at which thirty-one unions were represented, approved a common scheme of amalgamation. On the outbreak of war, however, the joint secretaries of the two bodies agreed to defer the amalgamation talks until after the war. In fact, the scheme was never taken up again.

At the November 1914 General Council meeting of the Gasworkers, it was resolved that, though they accepted that the war had stifled, for the time being, the ambitious scheme of amalgamation between the two federations, the Union should make individual approaches to other unions. And two years later, at the 1916 Biennial Congress, delegates again pressed for amalgamation with any other union 'of a like character',[9] while Thorne told his members, in the quarterly report of June of that year, that 'we have decided to open negotiations with any union willing to amalgamate'.[10] During 1916 and 1917, Thorne and Clynes made proposals for complete amalgamation to a number of unions, including the Dockers' Union and the Birmingham Gasworkers. Meanwhile, the other powerful 'general' union, the Workers' Union, was pursuing a scheme of federation with the National Amalgamated Union of Labour, by which a joint executive of the two unions, on which both secretaries would sit, and a common fund was to be set up but separate contributions and benefits were to be retained. The advantages of the scheme were that it avoided conflict over the leadership and that, because it was not a complete amalgamation, the law did not apply. The General Workers' Union, however, took the view that an amalgamation (in 1917, amalgamation had been made easier by a change in the law by which, provided half the members voted, a majority of 20 per cent or more would ensure success) was preferable to a federation and did not take part in the discussion initiated by the Workers' Union. Instead, they concentrated on negotiating full amalgamation with the Dockers' Union.

At first, the prospects for a union with the Dockers appeared promising. In his report to his union's Biennial Congress in 1918, Thorne told members that 'negotiations have been very friendly all the way, from every point of view, and in this way many difficulties were overcome'.[11] By December of the same year, the scheme, drafted by an amalgamation committee of the two unions, had been approved by joint meetings of branch secretaries and chairmen which had been held in all the main industrial centres. There was both industrial and political logic to an amalgamation. For the Dockers, amalgamation with the General Workers would have provided that union with a spread of membership which, in spite of its pretensions as a 'general' union, it did not have; for the

General Workers' Union, the Dockers' Union, with its membership in the docks and transport, would have given the joint union
a bargaining power which, on its own, the General Workers lacked.
In addition, the two unions shared a common 'new union'
tradition and Thorne and Tillett were old Socialist colleagues.

But, when the two unions balloted their membership in 1919,
not enough members of the Dockers voted to satisfy the legal
requirement. While the overwhelming majority of both unions
was in favour of amalgamation, only 41 per cent of the Dockers
voted, compared with a poll of nearly three-quarters for the
General Workers. The suspicion of Thorne and Clynes that the
ambitions of Ernest Bevin, the Dockers' dynamic National
Organiser, had frustrated the amalgamation were substantiated
by the voting figures for the Bristol Channel area (the largest
district and Bevin's stronghold) in which the proportion of those
voting was down to 27 per cent.[12] In an amalgamation, the leaders
of the General Workers, with three times the membership of the
Dockers', were bound to dominate the new union—at least at first.
Bevin, who had taken little part in the negotiations leading up to
the ballot, wanted more immediate influence and power through
an amalgamation of all the waterside and transport unions (which
he achieved in 1921, with himself as General Secretary). So an
amalgamation, which would have united the unions on which the
two great general unions of today are based, failed. In his 1920
Congress report, Thorne wrote, with a touch of bitterness, 'our
time and energy has been wasted'.[13]

However, other amalgamation schemes proved more successful.
In addition to a number of small and local unions, both the
Birmingham Gasworkers and the Federation of Women Workers
joined the General Workers' Union in December 1920. The
Birmingham Gasworkers, with forty thousand members,
strengthened Birmingham which, until then, had been one of the
weakest of the Union's districts. The accession of the Federation
of Women Workers was even more important. The General
Workers' Union had itself emerged from the war with a large
female membership. But it lacked the experience of and the
commitment to the organisation and the servicing of women
members which the Federation of Women Workers possessed.
Founded in 1906 by Mary Macarthur, the Federation had 6,000
members by 1910 and grew rapidly during the war; on amalgamation, its membership had increased to over 40,000 members. But,
as Margaret Bondfield, then Secretary of the Federation, wrote,

'it was ... a general union, competing with other general unions with women members in the same categories of trades'.[14] Its leaders, therefore, sought amalgamation with the General Workers' Union, which had about the same number of women members, provided they could obtain a special identity for the female membership.

In order to secure the amalgamation, the General Workers agreed to generous terms, including a women's department, under a Chief Woman Officer, a staff of women organisers, and a Women's National Committee, elected from a women's section 'to consider wage questions, propaganda service and all matters affecting the interests of women, and to make recommendations thereon, if necessary, to the General Council of the Union'.[15] In 1923 however (partly because of falling female membership) the separate women's section and branches were integrated into the geographical districts, and, in 1927, the Women's National Committee was abolished. It was only after the threat of resignation that Margaret Bondfield managed to secure complete responsibility for all national women's questions. Her reputation and her seat on the General Council of the TUC (she was chairman in 1923–24) ensured that it was the General and Municipal Workers' Union, above all other unions, that became known (sometimes despite its male members) as the Union for Women Workers.

Despite their setback with the Dockers, Thorne and Clynes were determined to pursue their goal of a giant general union. Thorne told his members in the new Union Journal that 'in consequence of the huge combines of big firms that are taking place, the general workers in all parts of the country, without making any distinction in any way between the class of work they do, should form one combination with a uniform scale of contributions and benefits which would be the means of preventing disgruntled members leaving one union and joining another, and would remove a good deal of jealousy that now exists in the Trade Union movement'.[16] Their next move was to approach (in January 1920) the federation of the Workers' Union and the National Amalgamated Union of Labour (NAUL), with the Municipal Employees Association (MEA) as junior partner, which had been created in 1919. An amalgamation of the General Workers' Union and the unions which made up this federation would create a great new union of 1,250,000— at that time by far the largest union in the world.

There was however, a major conflict between the philosophies and ambitions of the leaders of the Worker's Union, on the one hand, and the General Workers' Union and the NAUL on the other. Already, even though the federation had been expressly designed to avoid conflict, the NAUL had come to resent what it considered to be the undemocratic and overbearing nature of the Workers' Union.

The rise of the Workers' Union to an equal status with the General Workers had been meteoric. At the beginning of 1911, union membership was a mere 5,000. By 1920, it was over 450,000—probably about the same level of financial membership as the General Workers. The astonishing growth of the Workers' Union was based mainly on its strength in engineering, particularly in the Midlands. During the war, the insatiable demand for munitions had benefited the Workers' Union even more than the General Workers. In the two years after the war, the Union continued to grow, but, as its historian has pointed out, 'less favourable circumstances were to show that the foundations of the Union's achievement were weak indeed'.[17] Whereas the General Workers had just under a third of its membership in public utilities and municipal employment, which were relatively protected from the bad economic conditions of the 1920s, the Workers' Union had no similar haven and its largest group of membership in engineering was particularly severely hit by the depression.

Apart from its spectacular growth record, the Workers' Union was characterised by three other features—its exceptionally large number of officials, its centralised government, and its generous benefits. In 1920, the number of officials working for the Workers' Union was as many as 160, compared to the 60 officials of the General Workers. Though the General Workers' total did not include full-time branch secretaries, its policy was probably too cautious. On the other hand, the adventurous strategy of the Workers' Union, though effective in a period of economic expansion, obviously left it dangerously exposed and top heavy when the depression came. Secondly, authority in the Union was centralised in the hands of the General Secretary, Duncan, and the President, Beard, and a lay Executive; officials were appointed, the triennial conference had no policy-making powers, and district committees were no more than consultative. Finally, the Workers' Union which had, from the first, stressed the importance of benefits, adopted in September 1920 an unemployment scheme, which, because of its scale of benefits and of its offer of immediate eligibility to all who joined before December of that year, was totally unrealistic in a period of growing unemployment.

The National Amalgamated Union of Labour, one of the 'new unions' of 1889, had originally been a north-eastern union, drawing its membership primarily from semi-skilled and unskilled shipyard workers. In the 1890s and 1900s, however, the Union expanded among shipyard workers on Merseyside, Clydeside, and in Belfast and amongst surface workers in the Yorkshire coalfields. Like the Workers' Union and the General Workers (though, because its membership was more specialised, in a less spectacular fashion) the NAUL grew fast in the decade after 1910, and, by 1920, had 143,000 members.

In contrast to the Workers' Union, the ethos of the NAUL was 'anti-official'. From the start, a characteristic of the Union had been the importance it attached to shop stewards, which reflected 'the degree to which the office of shop steward was already being developed in the craft unions in the north-east'.[18] In some districts, shop stewards received payments for recruiting members and there is clear evidence, even before the 1914–18 war, that they were negotiators. The Union was run by an Executive of lay members, drawn exclusively from the central districts of the north-east coast. Though this may have made sense at first, by 1912 little more than one-third of the membership came from the north-east; and there was justice in the view of the Workers' Union that the union's system of government was anachronistic. The local Executive of the NAUL spent much of its time trying to keep an excessively detailed check on the work of its officials, who were, in any case, subject to triennial election.

Given the difference in philosophy between the Workers' Union and the NAUL, it was not surprising that there should have been conflict within the federation between the two unions. The Executive of the NAUL criticised the fact that one of the Workers' Union representatives on the joint executive, Beard, was a full-time official; it was worried by the number and high salaries of the Workers' Union officials; and, more fundamentally, it believed that the Workers' Union 'acted on the principle that the members should have no say in the affairs of the amalgamation, and the only use they had for them was to pay contributions and to provide the funds for other people to dispose of'.[19] They also accused the Workers' Union of poaching its members. When it came to discussing with the other two members of the federation the possibility of complete amalgamation, there was a further clash. While the MEA and the Workers' Union wanted the appointment of officials by the Executive, the NAUL demanded direct election. Thus, when Thorne made his approach to the three other unions, the NAUL, in particular, was in a receptive mood.

For two years, the four unions tried to work out a mutually acceptable scheme of amalgamation. During 1920, some progress was made by a joint subcommittee, and a list of agreed points was presented, in January 1921, to the four executives for their approval. The main items agreed were a large General Council (chosen on a district basis and composed of an equal number of lay members and full-time officials) as the governing body and, between meetings, a smaller executive (with two representatives of the General Workers' Union, the Workers' Union and NAUL and one from the MEA). Various amendments were made during 1921 to these proposals. The General Workers insisted on proportional representation as the basis for membership of the executive, while the NAUL asked for the supreme body of the new union to be a conference, a suggestion that was also supported by the General Workers. However, though both these amendments were accepted and an amalgamation scheme was agreed by the joint subcommittee and printed for the ballot of the membership, the attitude of the Workers' Union to the amalgamation hardened and, early in 1922, by demanding a ballot on the rules as well as the principles of the amalgamation, it forced a crisis in the negotiations which led to its exclusion from the amalgamation talks.

The underlying cause of the change in the attitude of the Workers' Union to the amalgamation seems to have been the catastrophic collapse of its membership during the depression of 1921. Its General Secretary, Duncan, wrote in his annual report that 'the year 1921 has not been a year at all, it has been a nightmare;[20] its membership was halved and fell to 247,000, while all its liquid assets were exhausted. The General Workers' membership also fell drastically but, with 356,000 paying members, by the end of 1921 it was by far the most powerful union of the four. Its demand for proportional representation merely reflected the realities of 1921, but, to the Workers' Union, it meant that the equal status, for which its leaders had hoped in an amalgamation, had disappeared. Though, even if the two unions' membership had been equal, Thorne's and Clynes' claim for the leadership of an amalgamated union was the stronger, Duncan and Beard,

95

always optimistic for the future, were not prepared, now that the Workers' Union had become so much the junior partner, to submerge their Union's identity in a larger union—particularly one, in which the power, according to Beard, would no longer be in the hands of the executive and the officials.[21]

Should Thorne have tried harder to keep the Workers' Union in the talks? After all, any large-scale amalgamation of general unions should have included the Workers' Union, with its key position in engineering, particularly in the Midlands. There are two pieces of evidence that seem to indicate that the behaviour of the General Workers was reasonable. On 27 February 1922, when it became obvious that talks with the Workers' Union were about to break down, Thorne, in a firm but conciliatory letter, wrote to Duncan pleading for a return to 'the common action which representatives of the four organisations were able to take up to the time the amalgamation scheme was printed', and assuring him that additional points raised by the General Workers (on benefits, methods of organisation, members of Parliament, and the political fund) would not be 'a bar to future progress in the completion of our efforts for amalgamation'.[22] It is also significant that not only the NAUL but also the MEA agreed to continue the amalgamation talks with the General Workers' Union, despite the absence of the Workers' Union. In contrast to the NAUL, the MEA had had reasonably good relations with the Workers' Union; but the fact that, after the breakdown of the amalgamation talks, it was the MEA that took the initiative, in a letter to Thorne,[23] in setting up a further meeting of the Amalgamation Committee, without the Workers' Union, suggests that that union shared the view of the other two unions that it was the Workers' Union, not the General Workers, which was acting in a high-handed manner. Thus the judgement of one historian that 'its financial troubles made the Workers' Union seem a less attractive partner to the NUGW and encouraged the latter to drive the hardest possible bargain'[24] is too harsh on Thorne and Clynes. The fact remains, however, that the failure to achieve an amalgamation with the Workers' Union was to cost the General Workers dear in the future.

Against a background of continuing unemployment, wage cuts, and disputes, declining union membership and depleted reserves, the three remaining unions were encouraged to continue their talks. As Thorne told his members, 'the mutual trials and difficulties which exist at the present time have had a tendency to force many unions in close contact'.[25] A further factor pushing the unions towards amalgamation was the conversion of the powerful Amalgamated Engineering Union (created in 1920 by the amalgamation of the Amalgamated Society of Engineers and several smaller craft unions) to the cause of industrial unionism. Early in 1923, the Engineers wrote to the General Workers to terminate their previous agreement not to recruit unskilled workers. The Engineers' new strategy was an added incentive to the NAUL, with its position in engineering now threatened, to bring the amalgamation talks to a successful conclusion.

The MEA's attitude to amalgamation was somewhat different. Its General Secretary, Peter Tevenan said, in a visitor's address to the 1922 Biennial Congress of the General Workers' Union, that he realised the impossibility of workers dealing with industrial questions 'unless they were all together, in the same way as capital was today'.[26] Founded in 1894 as a union for London County Council Workers, it changed its title to the Municipal Employees' Association in 1898 and began to recruit local government workers all over the country. Its success brought it into conflict with both the Gasworkers and the NAUL, who complained that its low contributions (which it was able to afford because there were very few strikes in local authorities) gave it an unfair advantage over the general unions. At their insistence, in 1908, the joint Board of the Labour Party, the Trades Union Congress and the General Federation of Trade Unions ruled that separate unions of public employees should be absorbed into other unions. The MEA, after a vain attempt to get round this by changing their union rules to permit the recruitment of workers in private industry, disaffiliated from both the TUC and the Labour Party. Their original decision to join a federation with the Workers' Union and the NAUL had been an attempt, which proved successful, to secure re-affiliation to the TUC and the Labour Party. With the withdrawal of the Workers' Union from the amalgamation talks, the federation collapsed; and it was a logical move for a small union (even though, because of its local government base, its membership had fallen far less proportionately than most other unions) to amalgamate with a grouping that included the General Workers' Union—the other union with a large membership in municipal employment. In addition, amalgamation with the General Workers and the NAUL would give the MEA the security and prestige it had lacked in the past.

In the autumn of 1922, agreement between the three unions had

97

gone far enough to ballot their members on the principle of amalgamation. In addition to the ballot papers, members were circulated with a strongly worded statement which argued the case for acceptance: 'Each union has a power of its own, but the merging of the three unions into one will increase that power. It is the natural development of the principles of organisation upon which each union is founded. Economy, both of effort and expense, will follow amalgamation. The energy which has too often been spent by the separate unions in striving against each other will be employed to the mutual advantage of all.'[27] The result was a majority in all three unions for amalgamation. Thorne was delighted. 'We can now hope and expect that the Amalgamated Union will be in full working order at a very early date', he told his members early in 1923.[28]

In fact, it took until February 1924 before delegates from the three unions finally agreed (at the Memorial Hall, Farringdon Street, London) on the rules of the new union. The amalgamation committee had spent nine months hammering out the rules, which had then to be approved by the executives of the three unions. The major issues were all thrashed out before the delegate conference met. Thorne and Clynes were to be Secretary and President of the new union. Bell, the respected General Secretary of the NAUL, had died in December 1922, and Spence, the corresponding Secretary of the NAUL and Peter Tevenan, the General Secretary of the MEA, were happy enough to become assistant General Secretaries. The officials of the General Workers' Union took all the secretaryships of the twelve districts of the new union, except for Liverpool, Sheffield, and Northern Ireland, in which areas the NAUL was the predominant union. As the MEA membership was spread over the whole country, it had no claim to provide any district secretaries (though J. D. S. Highman, a MEA official, became Leeds district secretary in 1925). The MEA insisted, however, that the new union should be called the General and 'Municipal' Workers' Union and that there should be a local government department at head office, under MEA officials. All existing officials of the three unions found jobs as organisers or temporary organisers—though with reduced salaries.

The institutions of government were closely modelled on those of the General Workers' Union. District officials were to be re-elected every two years by branches of the Union's districts. The final authority was to be a Biennial Congress (which became annual in 1945) of elected lay representatives. Between Congresses, a General Council was to govern the Union, composed of the district secretary and a 'lay' member from each district, with the largest four districts supplying an additional 'lay' member, so that there should be a 'lay' majority (a provision which satisfied the NAUL). The General Council elected a committee of five district secretaries and five 'lay' members (from the districts not represented by their secretaries) to serve, together with the General Secretary and the President, as an Executive. Thus, in 1924, the constitution of the modern GMWU was formed—a strong General Secretary, circumscribed by an Executive made more powerful by the presence of five full-time district secretaries.

At the delegate conference on amalgamation, which met from 12–15 February 1924, and was composed of 102 delegates from the General Workers and 52 each from the NAUL and the MEA, there was no controversy over the leadership and the government of the new union. Argument centred on the financial arrangements. As far as benefits were concerned, it was agreed to retain the MEA funeral benefits but to drop the NAUL accident benefit, until the new union's financial situation improved. The key issue, on which, by one of those strange quirks, the whole amalgamation suddenly turned, was a proposal to reduce the commission to branch officials by $2\frac{1}{2}$ per cent. Though officials' salaries were to be cut, delegates (many of them branch secretaries) argued that a reduction in their commission was an additional sacrifice for branch officials, whose incomes had already been diminished by falling membership. Thorne intervened to say that stewards would be willing to do the job even if they were not paid at all, but this view was not shared by delegates. Arthur Hayday, Chairman of the conference in Clynes' absence as a Cabinet Minister in the first Labour government, saved the situation by making it clear that amalgamation depended on acceptance of the financial proposals—and these were then carried by 59 to 44. Hayday, to sweeten the pill, then announced that, in the case of the collecting stewards (whose contribution was to be reduced from 10 to $7\frac{1}{2}$ per cent), the new General Council would, if the financial situation improved, give them first consideration for an increase, without waiting for a Union Congress to take place.

On 1 July 1924, the new Union came into being. Thorne had realised, after four years of effort, his ambition of a great 'combination' of general unions. Admittedly, it was against a background of falling numbers, so that the combined membership of the three unions in 1924 was well under a hundred thousand less than that of the General Workers alone in 1920. And the greatest prize of all, the Workers' Union, had eluded his grasp. But Thorne's achievement, and the sensible cuts in expenditure which accompanied the amalgamation, ensured the future of the General and Municipal Workers' Union as one of the great British unions.

Chapter 7

Aftermath

In 1924, Will Thorne was 67 years old. There is a strong case for arguing that, in view of his age, it would have been better for his Union if he had retired immediately after the amalgamation. However, he remained General Secretary for another nine years, during a period of crisis for the whole labour movement. For a younger man, the challenge that faced the Union would have been taxing enough. In his last years as General Secretary, Thorne's stewardship, though not without touches of the old authority, lacked vigour and imagination; his horizons had narrowed with age. If Thorne could have been backed by younger men, it would have been some compensation, but most of the district secretaries were also growing old.

The Union leadership's exceptional contribution to the Labour Party added to its problems. The formation of the Labour government in the last months of 1923 meant that the GMWU lost two of its most important officials. Margaret Bondfield was made Parliamentary Secretary to the Ministry of Labour and Clynes became Lord Privy Seal and Deputy Leader of the House of Commons (in effect, because of MacDonald's absences abroad deputy Prime Minister); both were unhesitatingly given leave of absence from the Union. Later, in Ramsay MacDonald's second government, 1929–31, Clynes became Home Secretary, and Margaret Bondfield was promoted to become Minister of Labour—the first woman to achieve Cabinet status; both were again given leave of absence. While the Union may have gained from having such a direct and, probably, unique link with the Labour government (the TUC bitterly criticised MacDonald for his lack of contact with the trades unions), the disadvantage was that the leadership lost, for long periods of time, both its best-known figure and the most effective woman trade unionist in the

country. Thorne, himself, remained in Parliament and was one
of the two Union MPs to survive the disaster of 1931.

For Thorne, 1924 promised to be a good year. The amalgamation that he had always advocated had been finalised on 1 July
and, as important, the first Labour government was now in power.
Stanley Baldwin, the Conservative Prime Minister, had dissolved
Parliament on the issue of Tariff Reform at the end of 1923. The
results found the Labour Party with the increased total of 191
seats, the Liberals with 158, and the Conservatives with 258 seats.
Although they were still numerically strongest, the Conservatives
had no overall majority; as there was now a majority against
Protection (Baldwin's chief election platform), they resigned and
MacDonald, as the Leader of the next largest party in Parliament,
formed the first Labour government, with Liberal backing.
Because the government had to rely on Liberal support, it was
obvious that no radical Socialist measures would be introduced.
Nevertheless, Thorne was delighted and reminded his members of
the close links that the Union had had with the early formation
of the Party. 'It was the agitation commenced by our Union
representatives' he wrote in the Union Journal, 'which initiated
political action on behalf of organised workers. Although no
really effective effort was made until the Plymouth Trades Union
Congress of 1899.' He went on to say, 'Twenty-four years count
but little in the world's history, and when we realise the progress
we have made since that resolution was passed we can look
forward to the future with every hope and encouragement. ...
Socialism gains ground daily, and in the application of its principles lies the hope of the human race.'[1]

Again, the Union was well represented, with twelve of its
members, five of whom were directly sponsored, in the new House
of Commons.

If it was a good political year, it was also a reasonable one for
Union members. Financial membership rose by 116,000. Although
most of this increase came from amalgamation, there was also a
slight increase in actual membership. Wages were increased in the
building industry, in the electricity and gas industries, and for
local authority manual workers. Indeed, the results of national
bargaining through the system of Joint Industrial Councils and
the co-ordination between the unions on the JICs was so effective
that the Federation of General Workers was wound up.

At the end of 1924, Thorne's hopes, however, were disappointed
by the fall of the Labour government and the return to power,

with a greatly increased majority, of the Conservatives. Worse was to come. Churchill, the new Chancellor of the Exchequer, badly advised by the City, had agreed to return to the gold standard as a method of dealing with the growing unemployment. The results were disastrous for the economy. By increasing the price of their goods, it damaged the export industries; unemployment rose, and the Union's paying membership dropped by 34,000 in 1926. But what was immediately critical was the effect of the Chancellor's action on the coal industry (in which the GMWU had members), which was already threatened by recovery of the German coalfields. As profits fell, the coal owners demanded a reduction of wages and an increase in hours. Instead, the government, threatened by the TUC with an embargo on all transport of coal if it supported the mine owners, reluctantly agreed to provide a subsidy for nine months, to end on 1 May 1926, so as to maintain the miners' wages. They also set up yet another Royal Commission to look into the future of the industry. Both sides, meanwhile, prepared for what looked like a bitter struggle.

Thorne vehemently supported the miners both in the Union Journal and in the House of Commons. In July 1925, he wrote, 'The mine owners want to take advantage of the weakness of the miners to force the abolition of the existing minimum wage and of the seven-hour day. To its demands formulated in that way the miners will offer an uncompromising resistance and I believe they will be entirely justified, the cost be what it may. My view of the miner who daily risks his life in the dark galleries of the mine for our benefit should be guaranteed to him a sum below which his earnings should never fall.'[2]

The Royal Commission set up by Baldwin reported early in 1926. Its main recommendation was that certain reductions in wages were essential if the industry were to survive and remain profitable. The Miners' Federation, whose secretary A. J. Cook was an old syndicalist, immediately came out with the slogan, 'Not a minute on the day, not a penny off the pay!'; and the miners prepared for a lockout from 1 May. The General Council of the TUC continued to negotiate with the government, as it had been doing for some time, on behalf of the miners. But, on a somewhat thin pretext, the meetings were abruptly terminated by Baldwin, and, on 3 May, the 'first line' of trade unions was called out and the General Strike began.

The government was ready. Most contingencies had been

foreseen, including the building up of coal stocks and the recruitment of a volunteer force. The unions, however, were less well prepared. The collapse of the Triple Alliance of 1921, at the time of the miners' strike, had left behind a legacy of bitterness in the trade union movement. Plans had been made in 1924 to form an 'Industrial Alliance' on a much wider scale to include iron and steel, gas and electricity, engineering and shipbuilding as well as the original transport, railways, and mining unions. Bevin, one of the main figures behind this new move, thought that only by presenting a united industrial front could the unions achieve the strength that the Triple Alliance had so conspicuously lacked. The constitution of the new Industrial Alliance, therefore, made it clear that once strike action on a national level was agreed the Executive of the Alliance would run it. Thorne and Clynes had misgivings about this project, because they feared it might lead to a direct clash with the government in which both wings of the labour movement would be the losers. The General Council of the Union held a special meeting to discuss the scheme. Both Thorne and Clynes spoke against participation, the former on the grounds that industrial action was not as effective as gaining political control through a new Labour government, Clynes because he felt 'in our case we should always find ourselves promoting the interests of others without ever being able to claim or receive the assistance of the Alliance'.[3] They suggested that strengthening the powers of the TUC General Council would be more effective. However, because most of the large unions were jealous of their independence, nothing came of the discussions. And the General Strike, in which the TUC had no power to settle the dispute, underlined the basic weakness of the General Council.

When the strike broke out the GMWU's surface workers were immediately involved and by 9 May slightly under a half of their members were out. However, on 14 May, the General Council of the TUC, whose members included Thorne, Hayday, and Margaret Bondfield, called off the strike. Faced with dwindling funds and aware of the government's intransigent attitude, they had decided that their cause was lost. The TUC leaders had received no commitment and no concessions from Baldwin, and, worse, attempted to cover up their failure.

Throughout the days of the strike, the members of the Union's National Executive kept in close touch, and a special Emergency Committee was set up, which included Clynes and Thorne. The

Union backed the TUC decision fully and was prepared to implement it from 1 May. This was not to say, however, that its leaders
believed that the General Council was right in the first place, to
call the men out. Clynes, in particular, never disguised his
disagreement. In April, he told the Union that 'such a strike
would be a national disaster, and a fatal step to Union prestige. . . .
A national strike, if complete, would inflict starvation first and
most on the poorest of the population. Riot or disorder could not
feed them, and any appeal to force would inevitably be answered
by superior force. How could such an action benefit the working
classes?'[4]

The Union held its Biennial Congress two weeks after the strike
had ended. Again Clynes stressed what he thought of as the
futility and pointlessness of the TUC gesture. 'Manifestations of
solidarity are admirable, but solidarity, without wisdom becomes
worthless, and the heroics of the first few days fighting fade into
the scared and subdued murmurs of defeated and distracted men.'[5]
As to Thorne, he returned to the theme of political action,
pointing out that it was the wage earners who had brought the
Tory Government in, and that they must 'now see that they are
paying a heavy penalty in more directions than one for being so
foolish'.[6]

The cost to the Union and its members was high. Thorne
estimated that there were over 127,000 members either entirely
without work, on short time, or directly affected by the dispute.[7]
As far as the Union's finances were concerned, thousands of
pounds a week went directly to the surface workers who, with the
rest of the miners continued to be locked out for a further seven
months—though the Union made it clear that they would not
support an embargo on the transport of coal which the miners
wanted. In total, £240,000 was paid out in dispute benefits.

Apart from the strike, one of the problems facing the trade
union movement at this time was the growing influence of the
Communist Party. At first the GMWU had expressed no ill will
towards Communists (partly, no doubt, due to Thorne's early
involvement with the SDF and partly because of the influence of
the left-wing London district) but, by the end of 1925, when it was
becoming clear that the Communists, under the umbrella of the
National Minority Movement, were determined to infiltrate the
trade unions the Executive took a firm stand. The District
Secretaries were circularised for their opinion on the NMM,
especially as to its affiliation with local Trades Councils, and asked

to report back to the National Executive. As a result of its survey the Executive resolved to have nothing to do with the Communist Party, to disaffiliate from any Trades Council that recognised the NMM and to give no financial or moral support to recognised Communists during the Municipal Elections.[8]

Thorne faced criticism for this decision. Immediately, the Glasgow No. 23 Branch (the Communist movement was particularly strong in Scotland) protested against the veto and a number of branches continued to support the NMM in the Glasgow Trades Council. The members of the General Council remained firm, and declared that the powers of a branch were subject to the higher authority of the National Executive and the General Council and that, therefore, individual branches had no right to take independent action. This ruling was challenged, however, and the Executive decided to go further. In February 1927, faced with a revolt from some branches of the London district on the question of taking part in a NMM Conference (which had been expressly forbidden), the General Council clarified its position. Any person, they stated, 'had the right to be a member of the Communist Party or the National Minority Movement and also be a member of the Union, but such person could not hold any official position in the Organisation.'[9] And the members, officials, and branches who had taken part in the Conference were suspended.

The quarrel with the Communists had an interesting sequel. In their determination to permeate all the trades unions, the Communists began to put forward candidates in opposition to leading officials. Though highly unsuccessful, such tactics earned them the wrath of Thorne and Clynes, who supported an amendment, which was carried, to the Union's rules. This amendment, which was brought forward at the 1926 Biennial Congress by the Leeds district, stated that officers, including the General Secretary and the President, who previously had had to stand for re-election biannually, should be granted permanent tenure, once they had been elected and had proved satisfactory.

The years between the General Strike and the formation of a new Labour government in 1929 were years of continued unemployment and reduced membership—very reminiscent of the last years of Victoria's reign. Thorne's main concern at this time, apart from trying to fight wage reductions, was the problem of the new Trades Disputes and Trade Union Act, introduced by the Conservative government in 1927 in reaction to the General Strike. The Act made illegal any sympathetic strikes authorised by unions outside the industry already in dispute, 'to coerce the government either directly or by inflicting hardship upon the community'. The rights of picketing were limited and 'intimidation' was also made illegal. An equally important clause was that which attacked the political levy paid by most trades unions to the Labour Party funds. Union members now had to 'contract in'—that is to sign a declaration that they agreed to pay the levy—whereas previously only those who wished to 'contract out' had to take any definite action. Finally, Civil Servants were forbidden to become members of any trades unions affiliated to the TUC or the Labour Party.

The Labour Members fought the Bill clause by clause in the House of Commons and the TUC backed this with an organised national campaign. The GMWU fully endorsed the General Council's opposition, organised factory meetings all over the country, and distributed literature against the Bill through every section of the Union. The President and General Secretary were particularly active; Clynes, with MacDonald absent abroad for some of the time, led the fight in Parliament against what he called 'the worst piece of vindictive and spiteful class legislation which our country has ever known',[10] while outside Thorne helped organise rallies against the Bill. What seemed most pernicious, as he told his members in June 1927, was its political section, which was aimed at reducing the funds of the Labour Party. 'The social reforms so urgently needed,' he wrote in his half-yearly Report, 'can only reach maturity through the ballot box; because so long as landlords and employers hold sway by a huge majority in the Houses of Parliament, then they will continue to legislate for their own interests at the expense of the workers, and resist any efforts made to safeguard the worker and elevate his standard of life.'[11] And, once the Act came into force, Thorne waged a vigorous campaign, appealing to all his members to sign the necessary 'contracting in' cards. In December, he reported success. 'In numerous branches the percentage of members who have signed the notices reached over 90, and in the Union as a whole up to the end of the year something like 80 per cent of the members have signed.'[12] Encouraged by a commission paid to branch officers, this high percentage was maintained for some years.

Thorne emphasised the need for concerted political and industrial action, as the one was useless without the other. The Act 'has brought home to thousands of workers that to rely on political action without industrial organisation, would be to their detriment, because many Acts of Parliament, the creation of the present reactionary Government hits directly at the workers' standard of living, and can only be resisted by healthy Trade Union organisation. . . .' He continued: 'I hope the workers will realise their limits of toleration, and make up their minds that indifference is not a virtue, and will get back into their organisation, and not only resist any such attempts of lowering their standard of living, but to consolidate themselves in their organisations so as to secure a greater return for the wealth they produce.'[13]

The effects of the Act were mainly psychological. Even though the sympathetic strikes clause was never invoked, the trades unions felt that the legislation was always a threat to them. Paradoxically, though the Act was designed to limit trade union political activity (it is true that the funds of the Labour Party were initially reduced by one-third), the unions' desire to repeal the legislation stimulated them to a greater political involvement than at any other time since the First World War.

If the Conservative Party reacted sharply to the General Strike, some of the more influential employers recognised that there was now a need for some form of dialogue between themselves and the unions. An independent initiative was taken by Sir Alfred Mond, chairman of Imperial Chemical Industries, who invited the General Council of the TUC, under the chairmanship of Ben Turner, to informal discussions which would range over a wide field of industrial problems. A conference between the two parties was held on 12 January 1928, and it was decided that the talks should be continued by a small committee drawn from both sides. Thorne was one of the seven chosen to represent the TUC.

The GMWU, shaken by the General Strike, undermined by unemployment and a reduction in membership, was more than willing to take part in the talks. As Clynes told the Biennial Congress of 1928, it 'is the business of Trade Union leaders to reconcile rival claims and adjust recurring differences in a manner to avert conflicts which usually involve both sides in some form of loss. To arrange peace terms, conference is indispensable.'[14] And Thorne, to still doubts over the advisability of the discussions, promised his members that he would not let them down. The TUC he said, were not negotiating with the employers, 'but only investigating certain problems of common interest'.[15]

However, in spite of good will on both sides, the discussions came to nothing. The informal quality of the talks was abandoned after 1929, which made discussion that much more difficult, while the slump and growing unemployment widened the gap between the two parties. But Thorne continued to believe it had been right to hold the discussions. Some trade union leaders, in particular A. J. Cook of the Miners attacked the principle of 'Mondism' but, given the traumatic effects of the General Strike, it is not surprising that Thorne agreed to participate.

It was in this barren period for trades unions that the first hint of criticism of the GMWU leadership began to appear. On a number of occasions, Thorne and Clynes were less effective than in the past. The weakness of the GMWU duumvirate gave the Transport and General Workers' Union, under its vigorous leader Ernest Bevin, the initiative in general union affairs. Earlier, in 1925, the two unions, on Bevin's suggestion, had agreed to set up a joint committee 'to deal with the elimination of internecine warfare, transfer, recognition of cards, etc'.[16] This inter-union Committee is still in existence today. Out of it came another proposal again from Bevin. He suggested in October of the same year that the two unions should amalgamate. A joint Committee was, therefore, set up to discuss a possible merger. Nothing came of the discussions, which were allowed to lapse after the defeat of the General Strike. It is perhaps a reflection on the Union's leadership that the initiative, in both cases, should have come from the General Secretary of the TGWU rather than from Thorne.

An even greater opportunity was missed in the case of the Workers' Union. By 1927, that Union was in a state of collapse, as membership and finance plummetted downwards in a vicious spiral. The Workers' Union, unlike the General and Municipal Workers and the Transport and General, had been unable to recover from the effects of the General Strike, partly because its membership was more exposed, partly because of its reckless benefit policy, and partly because it continued to maintain an excessive number of officials.[17] Given that its membership had common interests to the GMWU and that its desperate financial situation would have made it difficult for Duncan and Beard again to adopt the attitudes of 1922, Thorne and Clynes should, at least, have approached the Workers' Union and offered amalgamation. No move, however, was made and it was the imaginative Bevin who gained from the predicament of the Workers' Union.

It amalgamated with the TGWU, with the result that the latter became the largest union in Britain.

Thorne also failed to approach a small breakaway union from the Municipal Employees Association which had continued to recruit local government workers throughout the 1920s under the name of the National Union of Public Employees. Once again, a lack of initiative allowed a formidable rival to the GMWU to emerge in local government.

The leadership showed its inactivity in other ways. In 1928, the TUC, anxious at the overall fall in membership, decided to hold district delegate conferences and public meetings to boost trade union recruitment. The Executive of the Union, however, took the view that more advantage would be gained if the Union pursued its own recruitment campaign. No further action was, therefore, taken on the TUC's initiative. However the Union did make a recruitment drive of its own a year later—without any great success. And it is sad to find Thorne blaming the Communist Party's 'insidious propaganda and pernicious influence' [18] for the GMWU's fall in membership.

Finally, the criticism of the leadership, which had been submerged, came out into the open in 1928. The question of union representation at the Trades Union Congress and the Labour Party Conference was brought up at a meeting of the National Executive of the Union. During the discussions, the advantage of sending younger members to the Conferences was put forward, for they would 'then have some chance of establishing a reputation and acquiring development to assist them if and when they attained national responsibility'.[19] It was agreed to discuss this further at the next meeting. The leadership was active in the intervening weeks. For when the question was again raised at the National Executive (by A. J. Bailey, a former NAUL official) 'that we seek power from the Biennial Congress for the General Council or National Executive to select such additional representatives as may be deemed expedient',[20] the resolution was not seconded, and the motion, for the time being, was dropped.

Labour was returned as the single largest party in the 1929 elections, and Ramsay MacDonald, again with Liberal backing, formed his second minority government. It took office at a time of heavy unemployment, to which the workers hoped the new government would find some solution. However, the fact that it was a minority government made it difficult, though not impossible, for them to carry through any radical legislation. Many of its new Bills, as for example, the Coal and Pensions Bills, were so whittled down in Committee and later in the House of Lords, that they reached the statute books in a very much weakened form.

Meanwhile, unemployment grew to over two million. The Cabinet, anxious that its unemployment fund would be exhausted by the growing demands being made on it, and with no agreed solution to the central problem of unemployment, decided in 1930, without consulting the TUC, to establish a Royal Commission on Unemployment Insurance. Its report, published early in 1931, recommended increased contributions and reductions of benefits; to neither of which any of the unions could agree.

As the situation worsened, yet another Committee—on National Expenditure—was set up, at Liberal insistence, under the chairmanship of Sir George May. Its findings, made public on 1 August 1931, came three months after the collapse of the Credit Anstalt in Vienna. This bank's disaster had resulted in a loss of confidence in the financial system, and a drain of gold from London. The May report reflected the fears of the City and of the international bankers. It recommended heavy retrenchment in public expenditure and, in particular, cuts in unemployment benefits. The Cabinet, divided over this issue, agreed, on 20 August, to consult the General Council of the TUC and the National Executive of the Party. The General Council reacted strongly. It sent a deputation including Arthur Hayday of the GMWU, that year's chairman of the TUC, as well as Bevin and Citrine, which was emphatic in its refusal to agree to any cuts. Despite this opposition, Snowden, the Chancellor of the Exchequer, and Ramsay MacDonald refused to give way and, on 23 August, the latter resigned office. He was at once invited by the King to form a National Government, with Conservative and Liberal support. If MacDonald had hoped to persuade his own party to go with him, he was over-optimistic; only a few agreed to support a National government, and on 28 September, he, together with a small band of followers, which included Snowden, were expelled from the Labour Party. In the General Election which followed in October 1931, the National Government won 556 seats and the Labour Party was reduced to 46.

Initially, the attitude of Thorne's Union to the Labour government had been favourable. Clynes and Margaret Bondfield were

111

congratulated on their inclusion in MacDonald's Cabinet; the GMWU now had eighteen of its members in Parliament, six of whom were officially sponsored. The General Secretary had high hopes for the new government. 'The advent of a Labour Government', he wrote encouragingly in June 1929, 'inspires confidence as to the future; the Unemployment Problem is being tackled in the right way. Merely to rectify anomalies and remove injustices of the Tory administration of the Unemployment Act by admitting more to benefit would at the most be a palliative. But the Government are probing the root cause of this evil which has inflicted untold suffering to hundreds and thousands of willing workers. May their labours be rewarded. I am certain that any improvement in employment will immediately be reflected in the membership of the organised movement.'[21]

However, despite the Labour government, there was no economic recovery; and the Union had to continue on the defensive. As different industries pressed for reductions in wages, the GMWU officials engaged in long drawn out negotiations in the hope that they could evade reductions, which, in the final analysis, they knew the Union had no strength to oppose. Membership continued to fall. A feeling of hopelessness pervaded Executive and General Council meetings. A symbol of the Union's pessimism was the decision not to build a large London office block. With the decrease in membership, it would not be possible to increase staff—and there was no need therefore for larger accommodation.

Thorne now began to express his dissatisfaction with the Labour government. In 1930 he had set up a special 'House of Commons' Committee, consisting of the Union's six official Members of Parliament, as a channel of communication between the Union and the government. At the Biennial Congress in 1930, Thorne stressed not only its importance but also that the National Executive hoped 'by the establishment of this Committee to bring into play quite a new Parliamentary instrument which will prove of immense value to our members or groups of members where redress of grievances can best be gained through Parliamentary effort'.[22] He went on to appeal to the government. It was now over a year since the Labour Party had been in office; Thorne conceded that the government's lack of a clear majority was a serious handicap, but he criticised the Cabinet's handling of the economic and industrial situation. Not enough priority had been given, he told members, to such industrial measures as a Factories

112

Bill, or the repeal of the Trades Disputes and Trade Unions Act. He hoped that the government would not overlook 'the great interest of organised labour as represented by the Trade Union Movement. Our representatives on the Parliamentary Trade Union Group intend to make every effort to stress this view point at the earliest opportunity.' [23] It was a hint to MacDonald and Snowden that they should be influenced by other factors than the City. But there was no indication that Thorne had any better answer to mass unemployment.

Thorne's growing, but basically negative, disagreement with the Labour government continued. He had been asked to serve on the Economic Committee of the TUC and spent much time dealing with major industrial problems, in particular with rationalisation. It seemed to him that the government, although it had also set up its own Economic Advisory Committee, was not prepared to look at the alarming unemployment situation. The findings of the Royal Commission on Unemployment Insurance (on which Margaret Bondfield served as Minister of Labour) were denounced by his National Executive and by the Trade Union Group of the House of Commons (about 160 strong) who passed a resolution condemning the recommendations of the report. Thorne fiercely criticised the Commission. 'To operate the proposals of this Report', he angrily told his members in June 1931, 'by reducing rate of benefit paid to the unemployed would mean cutting down to the very bone the food supplies of hundreds and thousands of the workers and their dependants, who are the innocent victims of the vicious capitalist system, and thereby seriously impair their physical and mental efficiency.' [24] This was not what the Labour government had been elected for.

As the crisis of the summer months deepened, the Union's dissatisfaction grew and, finally, two days after the resignation of the second Labour government, Clynes was called in front of the National Executive to account to the GMWU. His position, he stated, had remained consistent. He had alway been in favour of economies, but only where there was an obviously wasteful expenditure, such as, for instance that on armaments. He told the Executive however, that despite the crisis he 'resolutely refused to give any support to any reduction in unemployment pay', partly because it would leave the recipients far below subsistence level and partly because it would give employers the best possible argument for a general reduction in wages. Clynes said that 'if the alternative was to resign he decided upon resignation rather than submission'.[25] The National Executive, having heard the views of its other union MP's, including Margaret Bondfield, who had personally been in favour of the cuts and who was therefore questioned closely, fully endorsed the action of the two ex-Ministers for refusing to enter into the new MacDonald government. The Union set about organising for the coming election.

The election results were shattering both for the Labour Party and for the Union. Of the twelve sponsored candidates, only Thorne, who was returned unopposed, and Jack Jones were re-elected, and the Labour Party was decimated. It was not, as Clynes told the General Council 'so much an election where people were possessed of their full senses, as we had a state of panic produced by conditions quite unparalleled'.[26] It was unfortunate, in one way, that Thorne should have retained his seat, for members could point to the growing anomaly of a General Secretary of a great Union who still had Parliamentary responsibilities, and whose Union membership had decreased by 23,000 in the two previous years. Thorne, with the disasters of 1931 in mind, again appealed to the members; it was essential he said, as he had on so many numerous occasions, for workers to join a trades union; 'it is up to him to forge the weapon of defence by industrial organisation . . . it is now up to those who have either lapsed their membership or have selfishly stood against the movement, to get into the unions and so assist to present a united front'.[27]

It was one of Thorne's last reports. Although he once more figured prominently at the 1932 Biennial Congress, his contribution was low key. By the end of the year membership had again fallen, this time by 26,000 in twelve months. The TGWU, swollen by its amalgamation with the Workers' Union, was now over 100,000 ahead of the GMWU. The rumblings of discontent which had been heard in the preceding years came to a head. Earlier, there had been a tactful move to get rid of Thorne when he was presented with a motor car on the occasion of his 72nd birthday. The gift, a recognition of his life long services to the Union and to the Labour Movement, would, it was hoped, enable Thorne 'to secure some little pleasurable leisure during the years that remained to him'.[28] If the General Council hoped that their Secretary would take the hint, they were disappointed, for Thorne made no mention of resigning. In 1933, however, his colleagues were in earnest. The Leeds District gave notice that its members of the National Executive intended to raise the question of the General Secretaryship. Thorne took the hint this time and announced his retirement the following month.

However, he stayed on in Parliament as a surprisingly active GMWU-sponsored member until 1945. He died the following year, aged eighty-nine, having seen in the first majority Labour government.

Chapter 8

Conclusion

Will Thorne, though a Socialist, was no theoretician. He was, above all, a practical trade unionist, whose ideas were the result of his own experience. It is, however, the combination of Socialist morality with hard-headed realism which makes his opinions particularly valuable today. Thorne was a man of his own age, but, on a number of issues relevant to our own time, he had something penetrating to say.

On 'militancy', he believed that a union should be a 'fighting' organisation. In the heady days of 1889 and the early 1890s this meant using the strike weapon, wherever he could, to force employers to grant recognition and the eight-hour day. However, even in this early period, Thorne did not support indiscriminate strikes. On the contrary, only if a strike were properly planned as part of overall trade union strategy, was it likely to be successful. Otherwise, it could lead to hardship for those on strike and a waste of members' contributions in a fruitless battle. With the employers' counterattack and the bad economic conditions of the 1890s, Thorne's attitude became more cautious: 'Better for the union to lose a few members . . . than have them on the funds for six months . . . and then at last have to surrender', he told his membership.[1] This was not callous indifference but the realism of experience. Nothing destroyed a young union quicker than an unsuccessful strike, as the collapse of the Union of Sailors and Firemen in 1894 showed.

Thereafter, Thorne's views on trade union 'militancy' became more sophisticated. Despite his conviction that employers and workers had conflicting interests, he was not averse to a mutually beneficial agreement with management. This did not mean he had abandoned the strike weapon; on the contrary, both at the end of the 1890s and between 1910 and 1914, Thorne was involved in a number of strikes—some of which were successful. But, increasing-

116

ly, he saw it as a last resort, something to use when all else had failed. As he wrote in his autobiography, 'my endeavour is always to get disputes settled without resorting to direct action; but I recognise that the workers must never give up the strike weapon, which is their greatest power in the ceaseless class war.'[2]

With the growing power of general unionism during and immediately after the 1914–18 war, Thorne helped to create a system of national collective bargaining, in order to secure lasting gains for his members. Though he was always aware of its limitations, his view was that, given relatively full employment, collective bargaining was a more effective way of improving living standards than relying solely on the withdrawal of labour. To Thorne, 'militancy' became as much a term for hard bargaining as for fighting pitched battles—though, if he had to fight, then fight he did.

Thorne believed that every worker should be in a trade union. This seemingly self-evident point is more radical than it sounds. Before Thorne, it was the consensus of opinion amongst trade unionists that, except in a few industries, some types of workers— the unskilled, the low paid, women—were impossible to organise. And, even today, trade unionists need reminding that the majority of employees are not in trade unions. If the trade union movement is to be fully representative, then it must give the same priority to recruitment as Thorne did.

Thorne's views on methods of organisation also have their relevance. A modified 'general' unionism is today the dominant principle of British trades unionism. In addition to the TGWU and the GMWU, two of the most powerful unions, the Engineers and the Electricians, both formerly exclusively craft, are now 'open' unions—in that they are prepared to recruit all types of members in a wide variety of different industries. The reason is that, for many unions, an 'open' as opposed to either an industrial or craft approach to trade union organisation has proved more viable in a period of rapid industrial change.

However, Thorne realised that, if general unionism was not to degenerate into a competitive struggle for membership, then it had to be accompanied by a policy of seeking friendly relations and, preferably, amalgamation with other unions. Federation and amalgamation were in fact part and parcel of general unionism, and, though he was anxious to persuade smaller unions to join his union, he recognised that the real gains in breaking down un- necessary differences between groups of workers would come from

117

the fusion of large 'open' unions with their overlapping membership interests—an insight relevant today.

Thorne's trade unionism was closely linked to his overall Socialist philosophy. The idea of a limited business unionism without any social and political objectives was entirely alien to him. He always realised that his members were more than workers; they were also consumers and parents, tenants and prospective householders, sick and unemployed, and all destined to be old age pensioners. Hence, his union's concern with food prices, with child poverty and educational opportunities, the provision of municipal housing, with the introduction of unemployment and sickness benefit and with the establishment of old age pensions. As a Socialist, he also considered that, if there were to be any real improvement in the standards of the working class, including its lower paid members, there had to be radical changes in ownership and the distribution of wealth. In other words, the workplace situation had to be considered in a wider political and social context. His union was, therefore, deeply involved in the battle for social justice, through the creation and development of an independent Labour Party.

However, despite the Gasworkers' deep political commitment, Thorne believed, as his disagreement in 1912 with Tom Mann shows, that his first responsibility was to deal with immediate shopfloor grievances. Though trade unions had to define their political and social objectives, these were better achieved through an independent Labour Party than through direct trade union action. A trade union movement that did not work with the Labour Party in Parliament and relied on direct action would leave political power in the hands of the employers. And there was also the danger that a trade union movement that concentrated on political action would neglect its workplace responsibilities and, thereby, lose its members' support—to the detriment not only of the trade unions but, in the long run, of the Labour Party as well.

In any case, as Thorne and Clynes maintained throughout the 1920s, direct action was likely to be ineffective. In most cases, the Conservative government would win—and the real loser would be the workers, who would have made all the sacrifices. As a convinced democrat, Thorne believed that society was more likely to be changed through the ballot box, by the election of a Labour government, than through industrial action for political ends. Both Thorne and Clynes also pointed out that, if the trade unions engaged in political strikes, their opponents would use this as an excuse to thwart the actions of a Labour government. Though Thorne was as aware as anyone of the trials and frustrations of having to suffer under the policies of a reactionary government, he thought that the dangers of taking short cuts outstripped the advantages.

Thorne's whole life was devoted to the struggle to achieve rights for the workers. In the deeply divided and unequal society of his time, it was natural that he should see industrial relations and politics primarily as a class struggle. But, at the start of the 1914-18 war, he was faced with an agonising dilemma. Were there any circumstances in which, despite their deprivation, the workers should give their obligations to the community as high a priority as their battle for their own rights? Although he was an active participant in the international working-class movement, Thorne believed the war did provide such a set of circumstances. Of course, during the war, his union was able to win some very important gains for its members. But Thorne never disguised his view that, to protect Britain from German militarism, workers had also to accept their obligations to their country. However, he always believed that, without far-reaching social changes, there could never be lasting industrial peace. As he said in 1915, he did not see how it was possible to harmonise fully the interests of employers and employees under 'our present system of production', by which wealth was so unfairly distributed. At a time when the relationship between trade unions and the community is a subject of much discussion, Thorne's own assessment of the balance between trade union obligations and rights has, despite the different circumstances, relevance.

On many of today's most debated issues—trade union 'militancy', trade union organisation and structure, trade union objectives, direct action versus the ballot box, trade union rights and obligations—Thorne's ideas, formed by a lifetime's experience, should not be ignored. Will Thorne is important not only for the contribution he made to the development of the Labour movement but also for the clarity and honesty with which he faced up to the difficulties involved in being a radical trade unionist and democratic Socialist.

Notes

Chapter 1

1 *General Workers' Journal* (July–August 1923).
2 *Correspondence* translated by Yvonne Kapp, vol 2, *Frederick Engels, Paul and Laura Lafargue*, p 330, Engels to Laura Lafargue, 17 October 1889.

Chapter 2

1 Quoted in: Asa Briggs, *Victorian People*, p 96.
2 Ibid., p 180–183.
3 Will Thorne, *My Life's Battles*, p 77.
4 Ibid., p 15.
5 Ibid., p 19.
6 Ibid., p 23.
7 Ibid., p 37.
8 Ibid., p 40.
9 Ibid., p 48.
10 Ibid., p 21.
11 Ibid., p 47.
12 Ibid., p 35.
13 E. J. Hobsbawm, *Labouring Men: Studies in the History of Labour. British Gas Workers 1873–1914*, p 164.
14 Will Thorne, *My Life's Battles*, p 54.
15 *Radical* (28 May 1881).
16 W. S. Sanders, *Early Socialist Days*, p 52.
17 Will Thorne, *My Life's Battles*, p 63.
18 Ibid., p 58.
19 Ibid., p 60.

Chapter 3

1 Will Thorne, *My Life's Battles*, p 62.
2 Ibid.
3 Ibid., p 64.
4 Ibid., p 66.

5 Ibid.
6 Ibid., p 68.
7 Ibid., p 73.
8 Ibid.
9 Ibid., p 75.
10 Ibid., p 76.
11 E. J. Hobsbawm, *Labouring Men. Studies in the History of Labour. British Gas Workers 1873–1914*, p 163.
12 H. A. Clegg, *General Union in a Changing Society*, p 9.
13 George Lansbury, *My Life*, p 69.
14 G. D. H. Cole, *Dictionary of National Biography*.
15 Will Thorne, *My Life's Battles*, p 76.
16 H. A. Clegg, Alan Fox, and A. F. Thompson, *A History of British Trade Unions since 1889*, vol I: 1889–1910, p 88.
17 Ben Tillett and Tom Mann, *The 'New' Trades Unionism*, p 14.
18 National Union of Gasworkers and General Labourers. First Half-Yearly Report (1889). Herein cited as Report.
19 Second Annual Report (1891).
20 First Half-Yearly Report (1889).
21 Will Thorne, *My Life's Battles*, p 80.
22 Tom Mann, *Labour Leader* (20 July 1889).
23 Quoted in: Chushichi Tsuzuki, *The Life of Eleanor Marx 1855–1898*, p 198.
24 Will Thorne, *My Life's Battles*, p 91.
25 *Star* (7 December 1889).
26 Quoted in: Chushichi Tsuzuki, *The Life of Eleanor Marx 1855–1898*, p 199.
27 Will Thorne, *My Life's Battles*, p 111.
28 Ibid., p 131.
29 Ibid.
30 Quoted in: *Labour Monthly* (1934 May XVI); Frederick Engels, *Arbeiterzutung* (23 May 1890).
31 Will Thorne, *My Life's Battles*, p 132.
32 Ibid., p 99.
33 Ibid., p 106.
34 Sidney and Beatrice Webb, Unpublished Trade Union Collection, vol XLII, British Library of Political and Economic Science.
35 Third Yearly Report (March 1892).
36 Fourth Yearly Report (March 1893).
37 Third Yearly Report (March 1892).
38 Sixth Yearly Report (December 1894).
39 Second Yearly Report (March 1891).
40 Third Yearly Report (March 1892).
41 Ibid.

Chapter 4
1   Quarterly Balance Sheet (July 1899).
2   J. R. Clynes, *Memoirs: 1869–1924*, p 64.
3   Sixth Annual Report (December 1894).
4   Quarterly Balance Sheet (September 1900).
5   Quarterly Balance Sheet (December 1897)
6   Quarterly Balance Sheet (June 1902).
7   Quarterly Balance Sheet (June 1904).
8   Quarterly Balance Sheet (March 1903).
9   Biennial Congress (1908).
10 Ibid.
11 Third Annual Report, Brussels International Congress Report (1892).
12 Will Thorne, *My Life's Battles*, p 152.
13 Arthur Copping and Moira Wilson, *Pictures of Poverty: Studies in Distress in West Ham.*
14 *West Ham Herald* (9 January 1892).
15 Will Thorne, *My Life's Battles*, p 177.
16 Ibid., p 173.
17 *Stratford Express* (26 November 1898).
18 Ibid.
19 Civic Union Pamphlets. No. 4: *The Labour Party on the West Ham Borough Council.*
20 Ibid.
21 Interview in the *South Essex Mail* (20 January 1900).
22 *Justice* (26 April 1902).
23 Labour Party Library: press cuttings on Will Thorne. Harold Laski, *Daily Herald* (2 June 1934).
24 Quarterly Balance Sheet (September 1897).
25 Trade Union Congress (1899).
26 Quarterly Balance Sheet (March 1903)
27 Biennial Congress (1904).
28 Quarterly Balance Sheet (June 1904).
29 *Daily Chronicle* (13 January 1906).
30 *Hansard*, Adjournment Debate, 30 May 1906. Cols 454–456.
31 Will Thorne, *My Life's Battles*, p 206.
32 *Hansard*, 20 February 1907, Col 928.
33 Labour Party Library: press cuttings on Will Thorne, *Graphic* (23 May 1925).
34 *Hansard*, 15 June 1909, Cols 804–806.
35 Will Thorne, *My Life's Battles*, p 207.
36 Chushichi Tsuzuki, *H. M. Hyndman and British Socialism*, p 203; Harry Quelch, *Social-Democracy and the Armed Nation.*
37 *Labour Leader* (4 September 1908).

Chapter 5

1 Executive Council Minutes (29 and 30 January 1910).
2 Biennial Congress Report (1910).
3 H. A. Clegg, *Union in a Changing Society*, p 68.
4 Biennial Congress: General Secretary's Report (1912).
5 Henry Pelling, *A History of British Trade Unionism*, p 133.
6 Biennial Congress: General Secretary's Report (1912).
7 Richard Hyman, *The Workers' Union*, p 38.
8 Biennial Congress: General Secretary's Report (1912).
9 Biennial Congress Report (1912).
10 Trades Union Congress: Presidential Address (1912).
11 Ibid.
12 Quoted in: H. A. Clegg, *General Union in a Changing Society*, p 72.
13 TUC Parliamentary Committee Minutes (18 October 1911).
14 Labour Party Conference Report, p 126 (January 1917).
15 J. R. Clynes, *Memoirs*, p 179.
16 Quarterly Report and Balance Sheet (March 1915).
17 Quarterly Report and Balance Sheet (December 1915).
18 Biennial Congress Report (1916).
19 Will Thorne, *My Life's Battles*, p 219.
20 General Council Minutes (June 1916).
21 General Council Minutes (November 1916).
22 Quarterly Report and Balance Sheet (December 1914).
23 Quarterly Report and Balance Sheet (March 1915).
24 Quarterly Report and Balance Sheet (September 1915).
25 Quarterly Report and Balance Sheet (June 1915).
26 Unpublished material: Beatrice and Sydney Webb, Trade Union Collection A, vol XXVII, 30 March 1914, British Library of Political and Economic Science—Letter from Will Thorne to Miss Hutchins.
27 Quarterly Report and Balance Sheet (March 1916).
28 Biennial Congress: General Secretary's Report (1916).
29 General Council Minutes (February 1916).
30 H. A. Clegg, *General Union in a Changing Society*, p 81.
31 Quarterly Report and Balance Sheet (June 1916).
32 General Council Minutes (February 1917).
33 Executive Committee Minutes (16 July 1917).
34 Executive Committee Minutes (28 and 29 March 1917).
35 A. J. P. Taylor, *English History 1914–1945*, p 84.
36 Will Thorne, *My Life's Battles*, p 191
37 *Cab*, 23 (May 1917).
38 Will Thorne, *My Life's Battles*, p 179.
39 Ibid., p 195.
40 Richard Hyman, *The Workers' Union*, p 92.
41 Biennial Congress Report (1916).

42 General Council Minutes (November 1917).
43 Biennial Congress (1918).
44 Quoted in: Henry Pelling, *A Short History of the Labour Party*, p 42.
45 *Hansard*, 16 August 1917, Col 1553.
46 H. A. Clegg, *General Union in a Changing Society*, p 89.
47 Labour Party Conference Report, p 160–161 (1919).
48 Biennial Congress (1920).
49 Alan Bullock, *The Life and Times of Ernest Bevin*, p 142.
50 Speech to British Association, Quarterly Report and Balance Sheet (September 1915).
51 Biennial Congress: General Secretary's Report (1920).

Chapter 6
 1 Will Thorne, *My Life's Battles*, p 90.
 2 Ibid., p 96.
 3 Seventh Yearly Report (December 1895).
 4 Third Quarterly Report (September 1896).
 5 Quoted in: R. Hyman, *The Workers' Union*, p 10.
 6 Quarterly Balance Sheet (March 1911).
 7 Biennial Congress Report (1912).
 8 Quarterly Balance Sheet (March 1913).
 9 Biennial Congress Report (1916).
10 Quarterly Report and Balance Sheet (June 1916).
11 Biennial Congress: General Secretary's Report (1918).
12 H. Clegg, *General Union in a Changing Society*, p 99.
13 Biennial Congress: General Secretary's Report (1920).
14 Margaret Bondfield, *A Life's Work*, p 60.
15 Ibid., p 61.
16 *Journal* (January–February 1921).
17 R. Hyman, *The Workers' Union*, p 127.
18 H. Clegg, *General Union in a Changing Society*, p 28.
19 Ibid., quotation, p 101.
20 Quoted in: R. Hyman, *The Workers' Union*, p 132.
21 Ibid., p 157.
22 General Council Minutes (31 March and 1 April 1922).
23 Executive Committee Minutes (15 and 16 March 1922).
24 R. Hyman, *The Workers' Union*, p 158.
25 *Journal* (January–February 1923).
26 Biennial Congress Report (1922).
27 *Journal* (September–October 1922).
28 Ibid., (January–February 1923).

Chapter 7
1 *Journal*, p 25 (November–December 1923).
2 *Journal* (July 1925).
3 General Council Meeting (20 and 21 August 1925). Special meeting to consider the proposed Industrial Alliance of Trade Unions.
4 J. R. Clynes, *Memoirs*, p 75.
5 *Journal* (May–June 1926).
6 Ibid. (July–August 1926).
7 Ibid. (November–December 1926).
8 General Council Minutes (20 November 1925).
9 General Council Minutes (18 and 19 February 1927).
10 J. R. Clynes, *Memoirs*, p 92.
11 Half-yearly Report and Balance Sheet (June 1927).
12 Ibid. (December 1927).
13 Ibid.
14 Biennial Congress (1928).
15 Ibid.
16 Executive Council Minutes (13 and 14 January 1925).
17 R. Hyman, *The Workers' Union*, Chapter V.
18 General Council Minutes (May 1928).
19 National Executive Minutes (18 and 19 April 1928).
20 Ibid. (3 May 1928).
21 Half-yearly Report and Balance Sheet (June 1929).
22 Biennial Congress (1930).
23 Ibid.
24 Half-yearly Report and Balance Sheet (June 1931).
25 National Executive Minutes (27 August 1931).
26 General Council Minutes (November 1931).
27 Half-yearly Report and Balance Sheet (December 1931).
28 General Council Minutes (August 1929).

Chapter 8
1 Sixth Annual Report (December 1894).
2 Will Thorne, *My Life's Battles*, p 217.

Select Bibliography

1. *Union minutes and Conference Reports*
Labour Representation Committee and Labour Party; Conference and Reports.
National Union of Gasworkers and General Labourers, the National Union of General Workers, the General and Municipal Workers' Union; Reports and Balance Sheets.
Social Democratic Federation Conferences.
Trades Union Congress Reports.

2. *Unpublished Sources*
British Library of Political and Economic Sciences
Webb Trade Union Collection. Section A. Vol XVII. XLII
Labour Party Library.
Correspondence.
Press Cuttings.
Newham Reference Library.
Public Records Office.
War Cabinet Papers, 1916 and 1917.
Trades Union Congress Library.
Parliamentary Committee Minutes. Microfilm.
William Caunt; Two MP's from the Gasworks.
Political Manifestoes.
Press Cuttings.

3. *Official Reports and Parliamentary Papers*
Hansard.
Royal Commission on Labour, CMD, 6708, 1892, IV.

4. *Newspapers, Journals, and Periodicals*
Clarion.
Daily Herald.
East and West Ham Gazette.
Justice.
Labour Elector.
Labour Leader.

Leeds Mercury.
Leeds Weekly Citizen.
South Essex Mail.
Star.
Stratford Express.
West Ham Herald.
National Union of General Workers; General and Municipal Workers' Union: Journal.

5. *Theses*
D. W. Crowley: The Origins of the revolt of the British Labour Movement. London Ph.D. thesis, 1952.
A. E. P. Duffy: The Growth of Trade Unions in England, 1867–1906, London Ph.D. thesis, 1956.

6. *Pamphlets*
H. H. Champion: The Great Dock Strike. London 1890.
Civic Union Pamphlets. No. 4. The Labour Party on the West Ham Borough Council, 1898–1900. 1910.
Arthur Copping: Pictures of Poverty. Studies of Distress in West Ham. Daily News. London 1905.
B. Grant: Beckton's Struggles.
Keir Hardie: The I.L.P. and All About It. London 1909.
G. Howell: Trade Unionism New and Old. London 1907.
Tom Mann: What the I.L.P. is driving at.
            The duties of Co-operatives.
            Regulation of Working Hours.
            What a compulsory Eight Hour Day means to the Workers. London 1886.
Tom Mann and Ben Tillett: Labour Platform: New Style.
                          The 'New' Trade Unionism; A reply to Mr George Shipton. London 1890.
H. Quelch: The Social Democratic Federation.
           Trade Unionism, Co-operation and Social Democracy. London 1892.
J. J. Terrett: Municipal Socialism in West Ham. A Reply to the Times, c. 1903.
Social Democratic Federation: The Times and Municipal Socialism.
H. L. Smith and V. Nash: The Story of the Dockers' Strike. London 1890.

7. *Autobiographies and Diaries*
E. Bernstein: My Years of Exile. London 1921.
A. Besant: A Fragment of Autobiography, 1875–1891. London 1893.
M. Bondfield: A Life's Work. London 1950.
J. R. Clynes: Memoirs. Vol I and II, 1869–1937. London 1937.

M. Cole (ed) Beatrice Webb's Diaries, 1912–1924. London 1952.
H. Hyndman: Further Reminiscences. London 1912.
Jack Jones: My Lively Life. London 1928.
George Lansbury: My Life. London 1928.
Tom Mann: Memoirs. London 1923.
W. S. Sanders: Early Socialist Days. London 1927.
James Sexton: Sir James Sexton, Agitator. London 1936.
Will Thorne: My Life's Battles. London 1926.

8. *Principal Secondary Works*

F. Bealy and H. Pelling: Labour and Politics, 1900–1906. London 1958.
M. Beer: A History of British Socialism. Vol II. London 1921.
Samuel H. Beer: Modern British Politics. London 1965.
F. H. Bellows: Socialism in West Ham. Economic Review, 1900. Vol X.
Carl F. Brand: The British Labour Party. A Short History. London 1965.
Asa Briggs: Victorian People. London 1954.
Asa Briggs and John Saville: Essays in Labour History. London 1960.
A. Bullock: The Life and Times of Ernest Bevin. Vol I. London 1960.
H. A. Clegg: General Union. Oxford 1954.
        General Union in a Changing Society. Oxford 1964.
H. A. Clegg, A. Fox, and A. F. Thompson: A History of British Trade Unions since 1889. Vol. I. Oxford 1964.
G. D. H. Cole: British Working Class Politics, 1832–1914. London 1941.
F. Engels and Laura Lafargue: Correspondence. Tr. Yvonne Kapp. Paris 1956.
E. J. Hobsbawm: Labour's Turning Point, 1880–1900. London 1948.
        Labouring Men. Studies in the History of Labour. London 1964.
        Trade Union History. Econ. History Review. No. 2. Vol XX 1967.
Edward G. Howarth and Moira Wilson: West Ham. London 1907.
Richard Hyman: The Workers' Union. London 1971.
J. B. Jeffereys: The Story of the Engineers. London 1946.
William Kent: John Burns, Labour's Lost Leader. London 1950
A. W. Lee and E. Archbold: Social Democracy in Britain. London 1935.
Hugh Legge: Socialism in West Ham. Economic Review. Vol IX. 1899.
John Lloyd: London Municipal Government. London 1910.
R. MacDonald: Correspondence. London.
B. McCormick and J. E. Williams: The Miners and the Eight-Hour Day, 1863–1910. Econ. Hist. Review. 2nd Series. Vol XII, No. 2 1959.

H. Pelling: The Origins of the Labour Party. Oxford 1965.
        History of British Trade Unionism. London 1963.
        A Short History of the Labour Party. London 1961.

E. H. Phelps-Brown: The Growth of British Industrial Relations. London 1959.

Philip P. Poirrier: The Advent of the Labour Party. London 1958.

B. C. Roberts: The T.U.C. 1868–1921. London 1958.

G. Shipton: Murray Magazine. June 1890.

A. J. P. Taylor: English History, 1914–1945. Oxford 1965.

E. P. Thompson: Homage to Tom Maguire. In Essays in Labour History. Asa Briggs and John Saville. London 1960.

Paul Thompson: Socialists, Liberals and Labour. The Struggle for London, 1885–1914. London 1967.

Dona Torr: Tom Mann and His Times. Vol I. London 1956.

C. Tsuzuki: The Life of Eleanor Marx, 1855–1898. Oxford 1967.
        H. M. Hyndman and British Socialism. Oxford 1961.

S. and B. Webb: Industrial Democracy. London 1897.
        The History of Trade Unionism, 1660–1920. London 1920.

Index